ANALYSING OFFENDING

DATA, MODELS AND INTERPRETATIONS

Roger Tarling
Head
Home Office Research and Planning Unit

LONDON: HMSO

First published 1993

ISBN 0 11 341080 8

CONTENTS

Acknowledgements

I would like to thank the many people who helped me in the course of this work. Several colleagues in the Home Office, Patrick Collier, John Ditchfield, Chris Lewis and David Moxon gave me access to their data sets and dealt with my queries. John MacLeod and Patricia Morgan resolved my computer problems, Valerie Costello typed much of the text and Hugh Robertson prepared the report for publication. I am extremely grateful to all of them for their technical assistance, support and forbearance.

Outside the Home Office I owe a special debt to David Farrington who, amongst other things, commented on earlier drafts, and to John Copas my statistics mentor throughout.

Summary

Research on offending is not new. Important systematic work was undertaken by the Gluecks in the inter-war period and research evidence has accumulated since then. Speculation and theorising about criminal behaviour goes back even further. More recent research, connected with the U.S. National Academy of Sciences Panel on Research on Criminal Careers, has added to knowledge and further stimulated the debate. Causes of criminal behaviour, policy prescriptions to deal with it and future research agendas including the methodological approaches to be followed are the key discussion points.

This book is a response to the Panel's recommendation for research on criminal careers and falls into three broad sections. The first analyses data on crime and known offenders in England and Wales and reviews the research literature on the factors found to be associated with offending. The second section reviews and extends the application of statistical techniques to analyse criminal behaviour and the third considers criminal justice policy, in particular the extent to which custodial sentences prevent offenders from committing crime.

Since 1955 there has been a more than four fold increase in the number of known offenders, that is, offenders cautioned by the police or found guilty at court. The greatest rate of increase occurred up to 1975 but there has been less of a percentage increase since then. Since 1985 there has been a fall in the number of known offenders.

Crime is predominantly a young male activity. For every one known female offender there are over five known male offenders. This ratio is similar in most Western societies. The differential involvement by males and females varies according to the type of offence; the male:female ratio is highest for sexual offences, burglary, robbery, criminal damage and violence against the person. It is lowest for non-violent property offences, theft and handling stolen goods (especially theft from shops) and fraud and forgery. Self-report studies suggest, at least for some minor offences, the male:female ratio is much less than indicated by official statistics but even for these offences, and certainly for more serious ones, males report committing offences more often than females.

The peak age of offending is 18 for males and 15 for females. Although the peak age of offending for both males and females is during the teenage years for most crimes, the average age of offenders varies by type of offence. Relatively more sexual offences are committed by older males (very few females commit sexual offences). The average age of offenders, both males and females, is higher for offences of violence against the person, theft from shops, other theft, fraud and forgery and drug offences. On the other hand, burglary, robbery, theft of and from motor vehicles and criminal damage are committed predominantly by younger offenders, especially males.

Group offending is more common amongst juveniles – only about one third of juveniles commit offences on their own. The extent of co-offending declines with age. About two thirds of young adults (those aged 17 to 21) commit offences on their own and about 80 per cent of those over 35. The extent of group offending varies by the type of offence committed and by the criminal history of the offender; robbery is often committed by a group of offenders but the vast majority of sexual offences and motoring offences are committed by an offender acting alone. Offenders are more likely to act alone as their criminal career progresses.

Many males commit crime at some point in their life. Of a cohort of males born in 1953 about 33 per cent had been convicted of a standard list offence by their 31st birthday. By contrast 7 per cent of females had been convicted by the same age. Other cohort studies conducted in this country found similar, or higher, participation in crime. The results have been mirrored in other countries, the U.S., New Zealand, Denmark, Sweden and Germany. Although most offenders begin their careers as juveniles or young adults, a not insignificant proportion start their career relatively late in life. Nearly a quarter of offenders in the 1953 cohort did not begin offending until after their 21st birthday.

Self-report studies reveal even greater involvement in crime by the population, but most self-report studies have been confined to young people and less serious offences. Generally, self-report studies confirm that criminal activity declines with age. White collar crime, however, which often escapes official statistics, is not generally committed by young people but by much older age groups. This is attributable to opportunity; young people do not occupy high status positions which enable them to commit white collar crime. Indeed evidence from the British Crime Survey which asked respondents whether they had committed certain sorts of crime within the previous year showed that older age groups were more likely to have committed such crimes as stealing or pilfering from work, fiddling expenses and evading tax or customs duties.

While many people commit crime at some time or other, for most their criminal career is short. About 45 per cent of *offenders* in the 1953 cohort had received only one conviction and a further 18 per cent two convictions. For females 64 per cent of offenders had received one conviction and 18 per cent two convictions. The average length of careers for all male offenders is 3.3 years and 1.1 years for all females. If offenders with careers less than one year (most of whom committed only one offence) are omitted the average length of careers rises to 7.4 years for males and to 4.9 years for females.

On the other hand, the few offenders who have extensive careers account for a disproportionate amount of crime. Seven per cent of males in the 1953 cohort, or 18 per cent of the male offenders in the cohort, accounted for 65 per cent of the convictions amassed by the cohort.

On average active male offenders commit about three crimes per year, but the rate of offending varies between offenders. Interestingly, although there are many fewer active female offenders their average rate of offending is not dissimilar to their male counterparts. Active offenders, both males and females, commit offences at a fairly constant rate for much of their careers (between age 14 and 25), but the rate of offending begins to decline thereafter.

The evidence suggests that the extent to which offenders specialise in the types of offence that they commit is limited. The probability that an offender, having committed a certain offence, will commit the same type of offence next time is greater than chance but not much greater in most cases. Thus the degree of specialisation is not particularly strong. The overwhelming conclusion is one of great variety and versatility in offending.

Factors associated with offending

Poor parenting leads to delinquent offspring. Weak relationships between parents and children, poor child rearing skills, lack of interest in children's activities or schooling and ineffective supervision have been shown to be related to 'troublesome' behaviour and subsequent delinquency.

Low intelligence and poor educational achievement are associated with known offending. A variety of tests and measures of educational performance and aspirations, such as behaviour at school, attendance, examination results and qualifications have been shown to be important contributory factors.

Having delinquent parents, siblings or friends and living or associating with offenders increases the chances of engaging in both known and self-reported offending.

People of lower socio-economic status are more likely to become delinquent. Studies of official offending indicate that social status, whether measured by social class, family income or the area in which the person lives, is associated with offending. However, self-report studies find less difference in rates of offending between social classes and suggest some qualification to this general conclusion. Certainly, for white collar crimes rates of offending may be greater for higher social groups as they have more opportunity to commit these crimes.

High crime rates amongst certain ethnic groups in this country seem to be explained by the fact that ethnic minorities generally find themselves at the bottom of the social structure. Once social status and other measures of social disadvantage have been taken into account, race is no longer found to be related to offending.

Offending is higher in urban areas. This may be due in part to a disproportionate concentration of people with the personal attributes described earlier. But over and above that, anonymity, greater geographic mobility and weaker community ties reduce informal social control in urban areas.

The causal relationship between alcohol consumption and crime is not clear. However, there is evidence that a young lifestyle which includes a great deal of drinking in pubs and clubs provides an important link between alcohol and violent crime and disorderly behaviour falling short of serious violence.

Research to date has been most successful in distinguishing offenders from non-offenders. It has been less successful in discriminating high rate, persistent or frequent offenders from those offenders who have a brief or limited involvement in crime. From the research evidence it seems that the same factors are at play but persistent offenders have even more extreme ratings on measures of adversity.

Once into a criminal career the best predictor of subsequent offending is the extent of past offending – the number of previous offences or convictions. Age of the offender is also an important factor.

Drug misuse also leads to higher rates of offending. Heroin users, in particular, commit property offences (but not offences of violence) in order to finance their habit.

Little is known about the factors which lead to desistance from crime. A change in environment or friends can be significant.

Statistical models of criminal behaviour

In order to understand criminal behaviour and to assess effectively different forms of intervention, multivariate statistical models are required. This report examined two such classes of models, survival models (which are appropriate for analysing recidivism) and stochastic models (which are appropriate for analysing the pattern of offending throughout a career).

Survival models, based on the exponential and Weibull distributions were considered. It was found that 'split population' models provided the best fit to existing data sets and also appeared preferable for theoretical reasons.

Little attention has been directed to developing suitable stochastic models in criminology. Of those developed so far, most have included an estimate of the probability that an offender will terminate his career after a certain offence. Alternatively criminal careers can be conceptualised as being of a certain duration with offenders differing in the length of time that they are criminally active. A model incorporating career length was developed.

Policy implications

Many people commit crime but, for most, involvement in crime is short lived. For these offenders minimal intervention by the criminal justice system is required. This policy has been accepted in most western societies with regard to most juvenile offenders.

Persistent juvenile and young adult offenders have been the focus of more recent policy debate. Increasing the use of imprisonment to counter crime, by incapacitating offenders, has been considered, in particular in the United States. However, research suggests that this is not a cost effective solution; it is estimated that to reduce crime by 1 per cent in this country might require a 25 per cent increase in the prison population. Policy has shifted towards greater use of community penalties, at least for property offenders.

Factors associated with offending, listed above, stress the importance of early life experiences and factors which may pre-date any formal contact with, or are outside the ambit of, the criminal justice system. Addressing these wider social issues is likely to be the most effective way of preventing offending. Future policy developments are thus likely to place greater emphasis on such strategies as training parents in effective child-rearing methods, pre-school intellectual enrichment programmes, and other ways of compensating for social adversity and of addressing the problems of crime-prone environments and communities. Pursuit of these policies will require the involvement of agencies outside the formal criminal justice system.

1 INTRODUCTION

Since the 1970s there has been a resurgence of interest in research on criminal careers. In the United States this interest was spurred by increases in the amount of crime in society which, together with the mounting evidence of the limitation of 'treatment and training' to rehabilitate offenders and curb recidivism, led to a reappraisal of what was known about offending and offenders. Particular attention was paid to the extensive body of research which shows that a small fraction of the known offender population is responsible for a disproportionate amount of recorded crime. It was argued that the general level of crime could be reduced if frequent offenders were imprisoned for long periods, or 'incapacitated', as they would be prevented from committing further offences (Wilson 1975).

In 1982 a Panel on Research on Criminal Careers was convened by the United States National Academy of Sciences, at the request of the National Institute of Justice. The Panel was given the task of reviewing the contribution of social research to increasing knowledge about crime and criminals including the feasibility of predicting the course of criminal careers and the effects of 'incapacitation' in reducing crime. The report of the panel (Blumstein *et al* 1986) is invaluable in clarifying the nature of four salient dimensions of criminal careers: participation (the proportion of the population known to commit offences), frequency (the annual rate at which active criminals commit offences), career length (the number of years the offender is committing offences) and the 'seriousness' of the offences committed. The panel called for further research to improve the understanding and measurement of each of these dimensions and for the development of analytic tools and statistical models.

This book describes my attempt to take forward the Panel's recommendations for research on criminal careers by analysing statistical information on crime and offenders for England and Wales collected from the police and the courts as well as information collected on large samples of offenders for a wide variety of different research purposes.

There are three parts to the book. The first part (Chapters 2 to 5) describes known offending, mainly using official crime statistics. Chapter 2 uses the annual Criminal Statistics to describe the extent and nature of known offending, how it varies between the sexes and between age groups, together with analyses of the inter-relationships between age, sex and type of offence. Chapter 3 examines participation in offending using evidence available from both official criminal records and studies of self-reported offending and makes comparisons with the findings of similar studies conducted in other countries. Chapter 4 examines the frequency and rate of offending and the length of criminal careers. A simple statistical model is produced to assess the probability of an individual receiving another conviction. Chapter 5 briefly reviews the research literature on social factors found to be associated with the duration of criminal careers in terms of initiation, continuance and desistance.

The second part of the book (Chapters 6 to 8) reviews and extends the application of sophisticated statistical analytic techniques to the data on known offending. Work on statistical models of criminal behaviour has grown substantially in recent years and will become more important in both increasing our understanding of crime and in providing tools for more effective evaluations of social and criminal justice interventions. Chapter 6 describes the application of survival models, Chapter 7 describes the application of stochastic models and Chapter 8 describes the calculation of transition probabilities and markov processes to examine the extent of specialisation of offences in criminal careers.

The third part (Chapters 9 and 10) considers the application of the statistical analyses of criminal careers to the development and evaluation of criminal justice policy. In Chapter 9 estimates are presented of the extent to which crime would be prevented by incapacitating offenders. Chapter 10 discusses the relevance of research on criminal careers for criminal justice policy and makes suggestions for further research.

The remainder of this chapter discusses methodological issues, the measurement of offending, cross-sectional and longitudinal research designs, and describes some of the data sets available for analysis.

Measuring offending

There are two main ways of measuring offending. The first uses official records held by various criminal justice agencies, the second asks people to report their own criminal behaviour (whether or not this resulted in official action). Both measures, *official records* and *self-reported* offending, have their strengths and weaknesses, as set out below.

Official records

The disadvantage of using official records to measure offending is that they relate only to known offenders, that is those who have been apprehended, admitted their guilt or have been found guilty at court. Inevitably they reveal nothing about offenders who are not caught or the perpetrators of offences that are not solved. In England and Wales information on police cautioning(1.1) and convictions following prosecution at court have been used to measure offending. (In other countries, notably the United States, arrest data are often employed.)

The extent of the potential difficulty in measuring criminal behaviour from official records is indicated by the data in Table 1.1 which shows the number of offences known to the police in selective years since 1955 together with the number and percentage cleared up and the number of offenders either cautioned by the police or found guilty at court(1.2).

Table 1.1
Recorded crime, number of crimes cleared up and number of persons dealt with: 1955–90*

Year	*Number of crimes recorded by the police*	*Crimes cleared up*		*Persons found guilty or cautioned for indictable offences*		
		number (000's)	*per cent of recorded crime*	*number (000's)*	*% of rec'd crime*	*% of crimes cleared up*
1955	438	214	49	120	27	56
1960	749	330	44	187	25	56
1965	1,134	445	39	246	22	55
1970	1,568	705	45	379	24	54
1975	2,106	927	44	505	24	54
1980	2,521	996	40	555	22	56
1985	3,426	1,212	35	587	17	48
1990	4,364	1,379	32	506	12	37

* 1950–1975 Indictable offences; 1980 Serious offences; 1985 and 1990 Notifiable offences.

Source: *Criminal Statistics England and Wales*

It can be seen that recorded crime has increased nearly ten fold since 1955 and the number of crimes cleared up by over six fold during the same period. The difference between the two is reflected in the decline in the clear up rate. Thus official statistics leave unanswered the question who commits those crimes (the majority) which are not cleared up. However, the number of persons dealt with expressed as a proportion of the number of crimes recorded and the number of crimes cleared up has stayed fairly constant over much of the period although both deteriorated in 1985 and again in 1990.

The fact that there is not a one to one correspondence between offences cleared by the police and the number of persons dealt with is attributable to many factors. For example, an offence may have been committed by several offenders or one offender may have committed and been cautioned or charged with several offences. Some offences are 'taken into consideration' by the court when sentencing the offender. The police do not always clear offences by cautioning or prosecuting a suspect. Rules exist whereby the police can count a crime as cleared 'otherwise without proceedings' where there is some technical or other obstacle to prosecution or caution (the offender may have died or may prove to be a child under the age of criminal responsibility or where further action may serve no useful purpose – the offender may already be in prison). A detailed discussion of how crimes are cleared and the contribution of the various 'methods' of crime clearance for each type of offence is given in Burrows and Tarling (1982 and 1987).

In addition to the shortfall between recorded crime and offenders dealt with, official records can say nothing about offenders committing offences which do not come to the attention of the police – the dark figure of crime. Victims surveys such as the British Crime Survey (Mayhew *et. al.*, 1989) throw light on the proportion of crimes victims claim to have suffered that are recorded by the police. Not all crimes are recorded primarily because many are not reported in the first place and some that are, are not recorded by the police for some other reason. The 1987 British Crime Survey indicates that the level of crime is somewhere in the order of four times higher than official statistics. The proportion varies greatly according to the type of offence; about 86 per cent of thefts of a motor vehicle are recorded by the police. At the other extreme only 10 per cent of offences of vandalism are recorded. In between, rates were found to be: theft from a motor vehicle 30 per cent, theft in a dwelling 42 per cent, burglary 41 per cent. Whatever the reliability of these figures they do suggest that there is a considerable amount of offending of which the authorities are unaware.

Even having accepted these limitations, other potential problems can arise when comparing official records *over time*. The most important issue here arises from the rapid increase in the use of police cautions since the late 1960s/early 1970s. In 1965 the cautioning rate (that is the percentage of offenders cautioned of those cautioned and found guilty) was 11 whereas in 1990 this percentage had reached 33. Thus conclusions about levels of offending based only on court proceedings will not necessarily be comparable during that period especially conclusions drawn about juvenile offending and offending by older persons and females, the groups most likely to be cautioned. Thus changes in official responses to crime may themselves introduce inconsistencies.

Another general criticism of official records advanced first by Kitsuse and Cicourel (1963) and Box (1971) is that they reveal more about the policies and practices of the agencies within the criminal justice system than of the behaviour of individuals themselves. Amongst other aspects of their argument they point out that the discretion available to criminal justice agencies enables them to determine, at least to some extent, who to target and hence who becomes labelled as delinquent or who ends up with an official record. Thus the offender population as seen in official records is the manifestation of a complex process of behaviour, official reactions and processes.

Self-reported offending

Because official reports tell only part of the story or a 'different' story, many researchers have attempted to measure offending through self-report methods. Self-report studies of delinquency can be traced back to the 1940s and have grown in prominence since then. Potentially self-reported offending overcomes many of the problems associated with official records but it presents its own set of difficulties which should not be overlooked. As will be seen when the results are presented, many self-report studies are confined to fairly trivial offences. Questioning people about more serious offences is much more problematic and inaccurate as people may well be less forthcoming about serious crimes that they have committed.

Non-response is another major problem and, as is often the case, it is the non-respondents who are perhaps the more important so far as measuring offending is concerned. Furthermore, research (eg Hindelang *et. al.*, 1981) suggests that self-report studies tend to produce less valid results for those groups who are known to have high rates of official delinquency. Sample selection may also cause bias. For example, a sample of school children may well miss non-attenders or persons in institutions. If both sub-groups are more likely to be delinquent the results obtained can not be generalised to the whole population. Recall and the validity of the responses pose other potential problems although there are ways of minimising or checking these.

There are other methodological issues associated with self-reports, such as the choice between self-completion questionnaires or interviews and the way questions are phrased or ordered. For example, the proportion admitting to virtually identical self-report offending questions in the first two British Crime Surveys (1982 and 1984) differed substantially probably due to changes in the format of the questions (Mayhew and Elliott, 1990). Confidentiality is another issue. A final point to note is that in the past most self-report studies have comprised only young persons. This need not be the case and later studies have included adults. Further discussion of the methodological issues surrounding self-report studies can be found in Klein (1989).

Relationship between official records and self-reports

In the past the relative utility of official records and self-report methods in studying offending has led to much heated argument. Proponents of each method have questioned the inferences derived from the alternative source. For example, early self-report studies questioned the sex, race and class bias of offenders revealed by official records. As Hindelang et. al. (1981) state "The researcher, like the theorist, is often forced to treat one set of data as indicative of criminal behaviour and the others as indicative of rather drastic measurement error... Once the decision is made, all virtue accrues to the chosen method and what were once problematic discrepancies suddenly become *evidence against* the disfavoured method".

This controversy has since subsided following studies which have compared officially recorded delinquency and self-reported offending for the same group. These studies have shown a good deal of congruence between them once methodological, measurement or selection biases have been taken into account. The consensus now is that the two approaches are complementary. The errors stemming from each are so different that the two measures can be used to check each other.

Methodology: cross-sectional or longitudinal studies

Information on offending has been assembled from a variety of research designs. Most have been cross-sectional studies examining a group of offenders selected at one point in time; for example persons convicted at court in a particular period or those who are the subject of a certain type of sentence at a particular time (in prison, on probation or released on parole licence). In many instances retrospective information on past events has been assembled and individuals in these studies have also been followed up over a further period of time. Studies of recidivism are examples of this kind of research. Information in *Criminal Statistics England and Wales* is cross-sectional; data on offenders dealt with during the year are presented.

An alternative methodology is the longitudinal or cohort study. Typically, a group of individuals born within a particular period are selected for further study. Longitudinal studies can either be retrospective or prospective (or some combination of the two). Cohorts may include non-offenders as well as offenders.

Information collected via either design can include details of self-reported offending and official contacts (arrests, cautions, convictions etc) as well as other social or background characteristics of offenders and non-offenders.

Each approach has certain strengths and weaknesses. Cross-sectional studies can be structured to include a wide variety of age groups and the information can be assembled relatively quickly. Thus the results may be more up-to-date and relevant to current concerns and issues. In contrast, many years will need to elapse before results from longitudinal studies, especially prospective studies of a birth cohort, become available, by which time important social changes may have taken place. Most longitudinal studies undertaken in this country are based on people born in the 1940's and 50's and thus exclude subjects from ethnic minorities. Furthermore, these particular cohorts reached adolescence at times of high employment and before drug abuse became widespread. The information they yield is therefore limited and can contribute little to current concerns, such as the effects of unemployment on criminal behaviour amongst young people, the extent of involvement in drugs or the difference in offending between different ethnic groups.

Prospective longitudinal studies are better placed to study self-reported offending over time. Subjects can be interviewed at regular intervals (eg.every 2 to 5 years) and asked about the offences they have committed. It is difficult to see how this information could be obtained retrospectively. Cost is an important consideration: longitudinal studies are likely to be much more expensive.

Given the advantages and disadvantages of each method, it is sufficient to say here that no single research design is preferable. Often evidence from each is mutually beneficial. The question to be answered will dictate the choice of research design.

Dimensions and terminology of criminal careers

The Panel on Research on Criminal Careers (Blumstein *et. al.*, 1986 Vols I and II) attempted to standardise the terminology used to describe criminal careers; it found a good deal of confusion in the previous literature. To avoid further confusion the Panel's terminology and notation are adopted here and are presented below. Unfortunately some adjustment is needed to accommodate the differences between the U.S. and England and Wales. In particular, data on arrests are available for the U.S. but not in this country, only data on police cautions and convictions at court. Therefore although the U.S. notation for arrest is adhered to, here it refers to persons found guilty at court or cautioned by the police – this is made clear throughout the report. The definitions also set out the key parameters of the criminal career conceptualisation.

Participation

This is the proportion of the population that has committed an offence, been cautioned or convicted. Participation can be separated into two constituents: *current participation* which is the proportion of the population who commit an offence in a year (d), or who are cautioned or convicted (b). The *cumulative participation* rate is the proportion of the population who have ever committed an offence (D) or who have been cautioned or convicted (B). Participation rates may be restricted to certain classes of crime; for example, the focus may be on the rates for minor offences or more serious offences or any more specific category.

Rate of offending

This is the rate at which active offenders commit offences per year and is denoted by λ. This may vary substantially between offenders; some commit many more offences in a given year than others. But an individual's frequency of offending may also vary during his or her career. There may well be periods of high activity but he or she may be much less active at other times. Similarly, some crimes will result in a caution or a conviction and the rate that this occurs per year is denoted by μ. If q is the probability of being cautioned or convicted following the commission of a crime, $q = \mu/\lambda$.

Total career length and residual career length

Total career length (T) is self explanatory and is simply the time between a criminal career starting ('age of onset') and ending ('desistance'). However, at some point in a career, for example, when imposing a sentence, it may be far more important to know the *residual career length* (T_R) which is the length of time from that point to the end of the offender's criminal career.

Seriousness

Offenders differ in the types of offences they commit and it is important to know how careers progress, whether offences become more serious throughout a career, the extent to which criminals specialise or whether offenders simply 'switch' between many types of crime.

The data

Various data sets were available for analysis during the course of this study. Information collected each year for the compilation of *Criminal Statistics England and Wales* on known offenders (that is those cautioned by the police or found guilty at court) made possible more detailed analysis of the relationship between age, sex and type of offence committed. From annual data sets the Research and Statistics Department of the Home Office has created three cohorts of persons born in four weeks in 1953, 1958 and 1963. The cohorts were analysed to examine participation in offending, rates of offending and to develop stochastic models. A study of 5,000 juveniles (males and females) born in 1963 and apprehended by the Greater Manchester Police provided further evidence on the use of police cautioning.

Further information on self reported offending was available from the first two British Crime Surveys. Unlike other studies which focused on juveniles the British Crime Survey asked people of all ages whether or not they had committed a range of offences.

Moxon (1988) collected information on a representative sample of 2,077 offenders (1,851 males and 226 females) sentenced at 18 Crown Court Centres in 1986 and 1987. The sample enabled further investigation of offence specialisation and the incapacitation effects of imprisonment. Information was collected on co-defendants and extended the research evidence on whether offences are committed by offenders acting alone or with others.

Ditchfield (1989) selected a sample of men released from prison on parole licence in 1983, 1984 and 1988 in order to examine reoffending on parole. A subset of 738 men was analysed here to estimate rates of offending and to assess alternative survival models.

Further details of each data set are provided later in this report, when it is the subject of analysis.

2 Statistics on known offending

This chapter takes a fairly straightforward look at information recorded by the police each year on known offenders (that is, offenders apprehended and dealt with by the police and the courts) in England and Wales[2.1]. The age and sex of the offender are recorded but not other characteristics. However, age and sex are two of the most important factors associated with offending; it will be seen that young people are more likely to commit crime than older people and males more than females. Other social factors are discussed in Chapter 5. Obviously recorded statistics do not provide information on offenders who are not apprehended. This information is only available from self-report studies which are discussed in more detail in Chapter 3.

It was shown in Table 1.1 that in 1990, 506,000 offenders (419,900 men and 86,100 women) were either found guilty at court or cautioned by the police for an indictable offence, that is an offence falling within one of the following broad categories: violence against the person, sexual offences, burglary, robbery, theft and handling stolen goods, fraud and forgery, criminal damage and a relatively small number of other indictable offences, the principal one being trafficking in controlled drugs. (A full list of indictable offences is given in Appendix 1.) The main point to note is that these categories exclude the vast number of less serious summary offences mainly comprising minor motoring offences.

From Table 1.1 it can also be seen that the number of known offenders dealt with has increased markedly; more than a four fold increase since 1955. However, the greatest rate of increase occurred up to 1975 but there has been less of an increase since then. Furthermore, the number dealt with fell between 1985 and 1990 which is due, in part, to the decline in the clear up rate and possibly to the growing use by the police of 'unrecorded warnings' rather than recorded cautions for apprehended juvenile offenders. Table 2.1 separates these data by the sex of the offender, expresses offending as a rate per 100,000 of the population and presents the ratio of male to female known offenders.

Table 2.1
Persons found guilty or cautioned for indictable offences and per capita (per 100,000 population) by sex: 1955–1990.

Year	*Number of male known offenders*	*Number of male known offenders per 100,000 population*	*Number of female known offenders*	*Number of female known offenders per 100,000 population*	*Male/ Female ratio*
1955	104.0	559	16.2	79	7.1:1
1960	163.7	850	26.3	112	7.6:1
1965	209.2	1,083	37.2	179	6.1:1
1970	323.7	1,644	54.8	258	6.4:1
1975	418.4	2,072	86.3	398	5.2:1
1980	459.8	2,200	95.4	427	5.2:1
1985	486.8	2,297	100.2	443	5.2:1
1990	419.9	1,962	86.1	379	5.2:1

Source: *Criminal Statistics England and Wales*

It can be seen from Table 2.1 that the number of both males and females dealt with has increased over the last 30 years. This is not simply a reflection of demographic changes as the rate of known offending (the number dealt with per 100,000 population) has also increased at least until 1985. Both the number of known offenders and the rate of known offending has declined since then.

Easterlin (1980), suggested that the number of young people in the population may itself disproportionately affect the level of offending. He argued that 'life' opportunities for individuals in larger cohorts are proportionally less. A large proportion of young people also places greater strain on those processes of informal social control and weakens adult societies' abilities to assimilate them. Both these forces lead members of large cohorts to become more involved in crime and members of small cohorts (where the forces act in reverse) to be less involved in crime than would otherwise be expected. Maxim (1986) analysed data for England and Wales for the years 1957 to 1981 and found some evidence to support this hypothesis; that the size of the birth cohort is related to the crime rate.

The increases in known offending have been different for males and females. For males there has been a four fold increase in the number dealt with but the rate per 100,000 population of offending has not increased by quite the same amount; an approximately three and a half fold increase during the period. For females the number dealt with has increased by a greater amount, more than five fold, and the increase in the rate has increased 4.8 fold. Thus the ratio of males to females has fallen from 7.1:1 in 1955 to 5.2:1 in 1990 (although it has been constant since 1975); this being due to the disproportionate increase in female offending.

Data gathered in the course of the three surveys conducted by the United Nations (Pease and Hukkila, 1990) provides some comparative information on offending in other countries. From the returns submitted by participating countries it is interesting to note that the ratio of males to females apprehended for crimes is broadly in line with the ratio for England and Wales. For example, countries such as Canada, France, Germany, Sweden and the United States have ratios for 1985 in the range 4:1 to 6:1. Furthermore, for most of these countries the range has narrowed slightly during the previous decade.

Type of offence

Table 2.2 shows the type of offences committed by known offenders in 1990.

From the first two columns of Table 2.2 it can be seen that the majority of offences committed by both males and females are theft and handling stolen goods - overwhelmingly so for females. A greater percentage of male offenders committed burglary, other indictable offences (which includes indictable motoring offences) and offences of violence against the person. The differential involvement by males and females in crime varies greatly according to the type of crime (the last column of Table 2.2). The extreme is sexual offences; but the ratio is also high for burglary, robbery, other indictable offences, criminal damage, violence against the person and drug offences. It is for the non-violent property offences (theft and handling stolen goods and fraud and forgery) that the ratio is at its lowest. In fact, for shoplifting (a specific crime within the theft and handling stolen goods category) the ratio of males to females is as low as 1.7:1.

Table 2.2
Offenders found guilty or cautioned for indictable offences by sex and type of offence: 1990

Type of offence	*Male[1] known offenders per cent*	*Female known offenders per cent*	*Males known offenders per 100,000 pop.*	*Female known offenders per 100,000 pop.*	*Male/ female ratio*
Violence against the person	14	10	283	38	7:1
Sexual offences	2	*	46	0.4	105:1
Burglary	13	3	258	12	22:1
Robbery	1	*	24	1	18:1
Theft and handling stolen goods	41	69	816	261	3:1
Fraud and forgery	5	7	95	27	4:1
Criminal damage	3	2	65	6	11:1
Drugs	9	5	182	18	10:1
Other indictable offences	10	4	206	15	14:1
Total	100	100	1,977	379	5.2:1

1. Other offenders, that is, companies, public bodies, etc are included with males and account for the slight discrepancy in the total rate per 100,000 of male known offenders compared with Table 2.1
* less than 0.5 per cent

Age of offenders

The age of known offenders is available from police recorded statistics and Figure 2.1 illustrates for both males and females for 1990 the rate of offending per 100,000 population for each age.

Figure 2.1

Persons found guilty at all courts or cautioned for indictable offences by age:1990

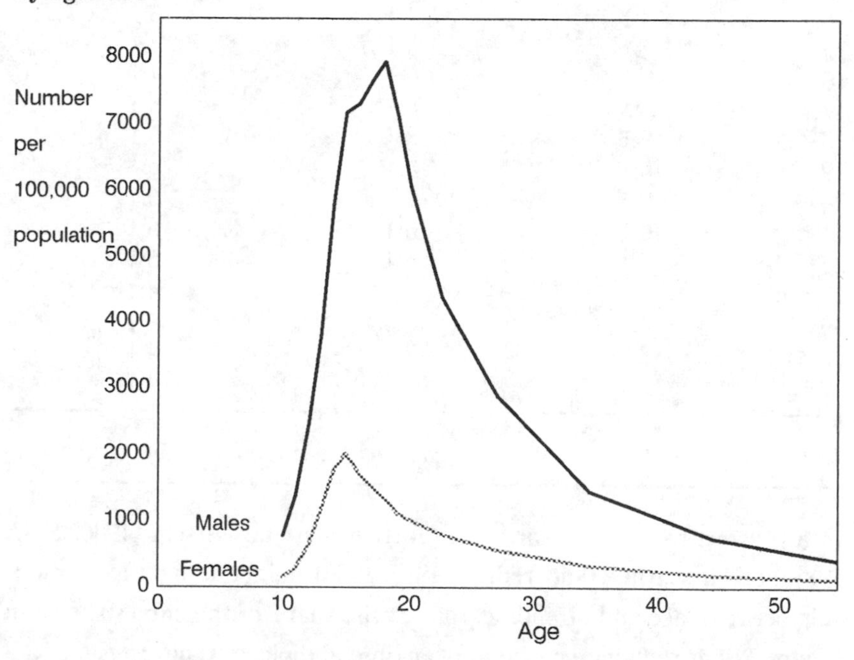

It can be seen that offending increases rapidly to a peak in the mid-teens and declines thereafter. The shape of the age-crime curve is rather different for males and females. For males the rate of offending rises to a peak at age 18 and declines thereafter. For females the peak age was 15 in 1990, but the rate declines during the late teens then falls at a much slower rate thereafter. This difference is reflected in Table 2.3 where the male/female ratio is generally lower for the younger and older ages but is at its greatest in the late teens and early 20s.

Table 2.3 also shows that the male/female ratio has fallen substantially since 1960 for most age groups but much less so for those aged 30 and over. In fact it remained unchanged for the group aged between 40 and 50 and actually increased for those over 50.

Table 2.3
Ratio of male to female known offenders by age: 1960–1990

Age	*1960*	*1975*	*1990*
8	14:1	–	–
9	12:1	–	–
10	11:1	5:1	5:1
11	9:1	4:1	5:1
12	9:1	4:1	4:1
13	8:1	4:1	3:1
14	8:1	4:1	3:1
15	7:1	5:1	4:1
16	9:1	6:1	4:1
17	8:1	8:1	5:1
18	9:1	8:1	6:1
19	10:1	8:1	6:1
20	9:1	7:1	6:1
21 < 25	10:1	6:1	6:1
25 < 30	8:1	5:1	5:1
30 < 40	6:1	4:1	4:1
40 < 50	4:1	3:1	4:1
50 < 60	2:1	2:1	4:1
60 +	2:1	2:1	3:1
Total	7.6:1	5.2:1	5.2:1

In a provocative series of articles, Gottfredson and Hirschi (1986, 1987, 1988) and Hirschi and Gottfredson (1983, 1986), point out that the relationship between age and offending, that is, the shape of the curves shown in Figure 2.1 has remained constant over time and place. They present data for England and Wales for 1842, 1908 and 1965 and for the US for 1977 and 1983. They also point to data for other countries, Argentina, France, Sweden and Japan. All the evidence reveals a similar pattern – a rapid rise to a peak rate of offending in the mid–teens and a decline thereafter. This led them to conclude that the relationship between age and offending is invariant over time, place, type of crime and sex.

Farrington (1986), in particular, challenges their proposition. He presents data to show that while the aggregate age–crime curves are similar in some respects they do vary between males and females (as was discussed above in connection with Figure 2.1) and over time (comparing data for 1938, 1961 and 1983 he shows that the curves have become more 'peaked'). Some of the changes that have occurred over time may well be due to changes in enforcement practice. Farrington was also able to show how the age–crime curves varied between types of offence, but in the absence of data for England and Wales, he had to rely on U.S. data. (See also Wilson and Herrnstein, 1985, for U.S. data.) A special analysis of the 1986 criminal statistics data permitted such comparisons for England and Wales. The results of this analysis are presented below.

Age of offenders by offence and sex

Separate curves were plotted for both male and female known offenders for a number of different offences. The separate offences considered are shown in Table 2.4 together with the peak age, the rate per 100,000 population at the peak age and the mean age of offenders. The analysis enabled some of the broader offence categories, such as sexual offences and theft and handling stolen goods, to be disaggregated into more specific types of offence. A selection of the graphs are shown in Figures 2.2 to 2.5.

Table 2.4 and the subsequent graphs reveal interesting patterns. It can be seen that the peak age of offending for males and females for all types of offence considered here[2.2] occur during the teenage years with a few exceptions (fraud and forgery and drugs) at 20 or 21. However, the exact peak age and the shape of the curves varies somewhat by offence. Sexual offences committed by males (few are committed by females and are not presented) show a distinct distribution - see Figure 2.2. The rate for older age groups is relatively high and this is reflected in the high mean age (late 20s or 30s) of offenders for the three sexual offences, rape, indecent assault and other sexual offences.

For males and females the remaining offences tend to fall into two broad groups. Burglary, robbery, theft from motor vehicles, theft of motor vehicles and criminal damage (at least for males) are more 'peaked' in that rates of offending increase and decline rapidly (Figure 2.3 is a typical example of the distribution for this group of offences). The mean age of offending is low and not too dissimilar from the peak age for all offences shown in Figure 2.1. A larger proportion of these offences are committed by younger persons. The second group consists of offences of violence against the person (at least for males), theft from shops, other theft, fraud and forgery and drug offences. The characteristic of this group (see Figures 2.4 and 2.5) is that while the peak rate of offending occurs at younger ages (in the case of theft from shops - youngest of all) the decline in offending with age is less marked especially at the older age groups. The mean age of offending is higher, reflecting the fact that more offences are committed by older persons.

Table 2.4
Peak age, rate of known offending at peak age and mean age, by type of offence and sex: 1986

Type of Offence	*Males*			*Females*		
	Peak age	*Rate per 100,000 pop. at peak age*	*Mean age*	*Peak age*	*Rate per 100,000 pop. at peak age*	*Mean age*
Violence against the person	18	899	24.5	15	152	22.8
Rape	18	12	27.6	--	--	--
Indecent assault	15	59	29.7	--	--	--
Other sexual offences	16	81	30.5	--	--	--
Burglary	17	1,759	20.3	16	69	19.6
Robbery	17	136	21.4	16	10	20.9
Theft from shops	14	1,888	25.3	14	1,383	25.6
Theft from motor vehicles	18	410	19.8	17	7	20.8
Theft of motor vehicles	17	1,058	18.9	17	39	18.7
Other theft	17	1,620	23.9	18	291	24.8
Fraud and forgery	20	267	28.1	19	102	26.4
Criminal damage	18	284	21.4	15	305	25.2
Drugs offences	20	276	26.1	21	44	26.3

When comparing males and females within each offence what is striking is the similarity between them, the only exceptions being offences against the person and criminal damage. For all other offences where comparisons can be made (that is, omitting sexual offences) the peak age, the mean age and the shape of the curve are remarkably similar although, being based on small numbers, the graphs for females appear less smooth. However, as discussed earlier, the absolute rate of offending is very different; females are much less likely to commit certain types of offences such as burglary, robbery and theft of and from motor vehicles. Yet these are the first group of offences mentioned above which have the characteristic of being committed by younger people. Put another way, the difference between the shape of the aggregate age–crime curves for males and females, Figure 2.1, (which showed that on average female offenders are older) stems from the fact that females are more inclined to commit those sorts of offences which are committed by older people rather than that females commit a similar range of offences as their male counterparts but commit them later in life. Furthermore, the higher male to female ratio in offending in the late teens early 20s shown in Table 2.3 is due to the fact that males are more likely than females to commit those types of offences which are committed by younger persons.

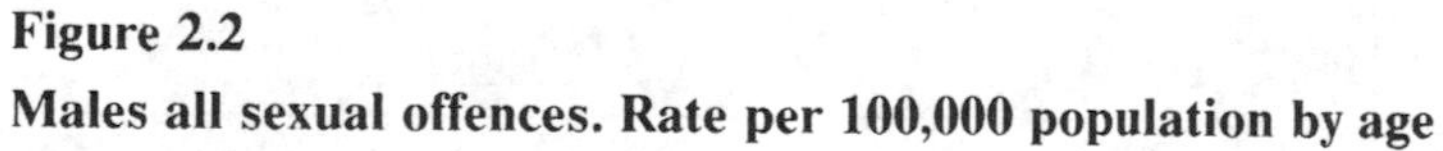

Figure 2.2
Males all sexual offences. Rate per 100,000 population by age

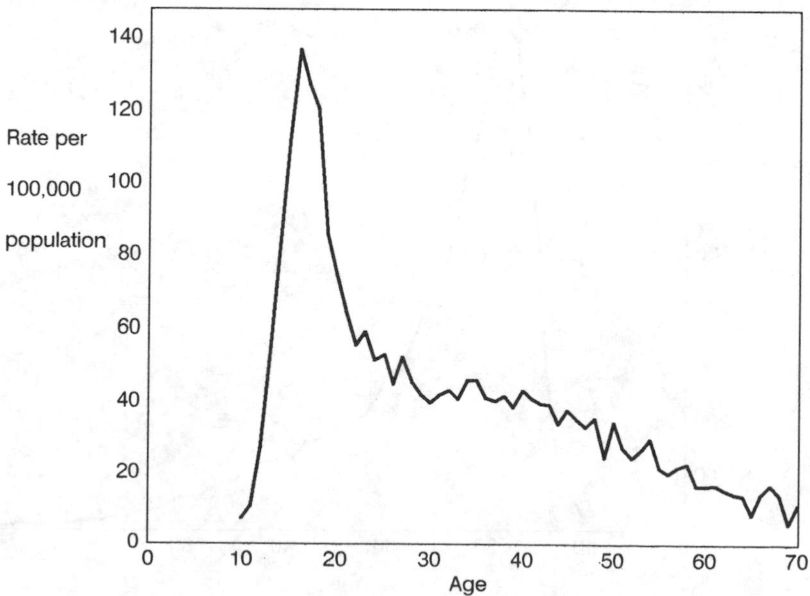

Figure 2.3

Males burglary. Rate per 100,000 population by age

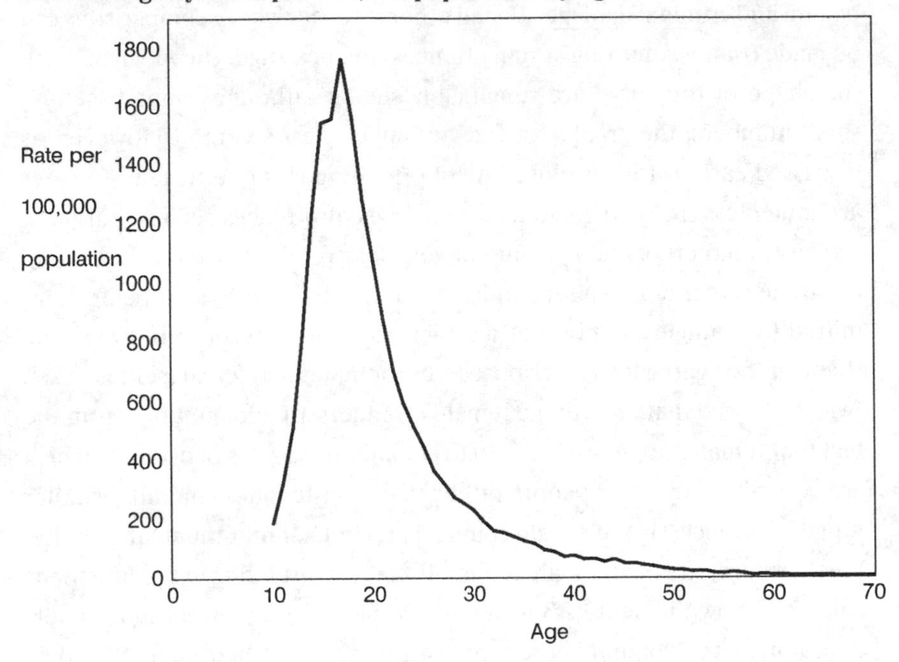

Figure 2.4

Males violence against the person. Rate per 100,000 population by age

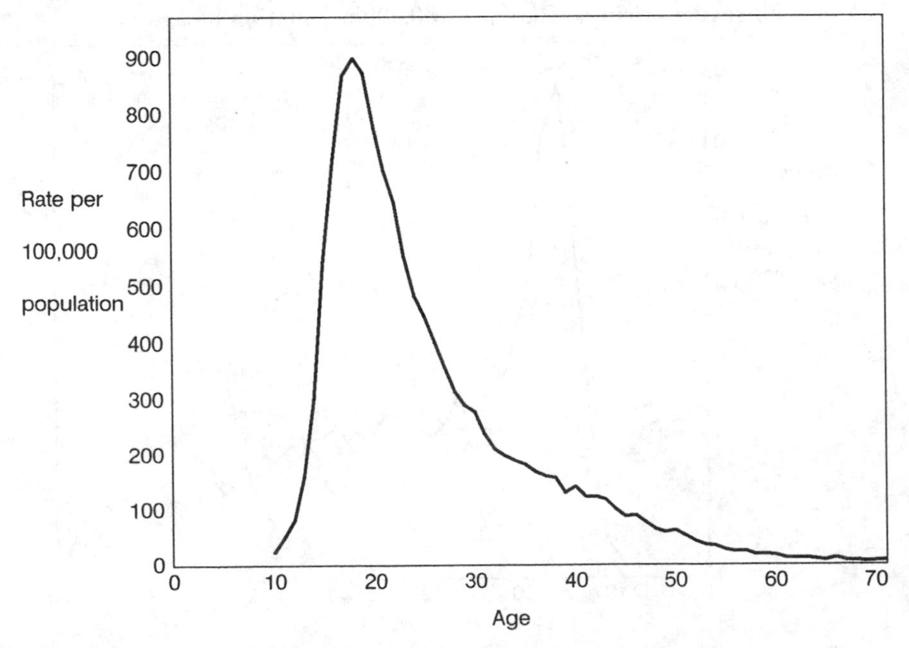

Figure 2.5

Males fraud and forgery. Rate per 100,000 population by age.

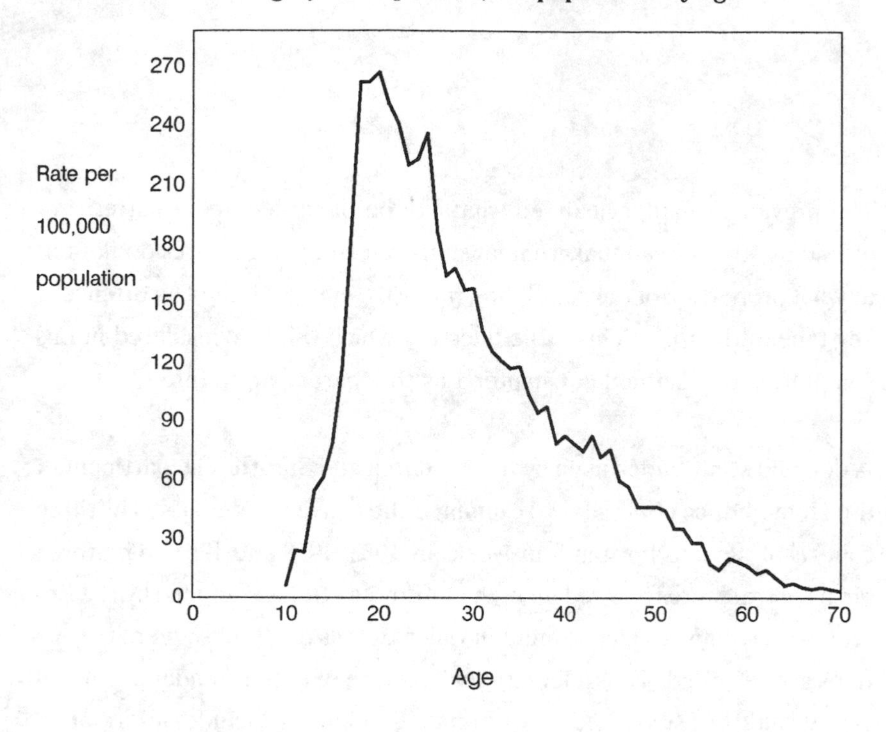

3 Participation in offending

The previous Chapter analysed what can be discerned about patterns of offending from the annual criminal statistics. But these figures do not tell us what proportion of the population (male or female) commit an offence at any time in their life. This is the question which will be considered in this Chapter. It was defined in Chapter 1 as the 'participation rate'.

A detailed study undertaken by the Research and Statistics Department of the Home Office (1985, 1989b) examined the convictions amassed by three cohorts of persons born in four weeks in 1953, 1958 and 1963. The three birth cohorts were followed up in the Offenders Index compiled by the Research and Statistics Department in which details of all subsequent convictions are recorded. Thus a longitudinal picture of each offender's criminal career could be established. The Offenders Index also includes information on the type of offence committed as well as the age of the offender at each conviction. Offence coverage includes all 'standard list' offences. Standard list is a slightly wider category of offences than indictable offences but for most practical purposes they can be considered as the same. (Both exclude the vast number of minor, mainly motoring, offences. Appendix 1 lists the individual offences included in the standard list.) At the time of this study each cohort had been followed up until 1984, so for the 1953 cohort information on offending was available up to age 31, for the 1958 cohort up to age 26 and for the 1963 cohort up to age 21.

The data for males and females are given in Table 3.1 and are presented graphically in Figure 3.1. They show the cumulative per cent of the cohort who had received a conviction by a particular age.

It can be seen from the table that males born in 1953 were followed up until their 31st birthday by which time 32.6 per cent had been convicted of a standard list offence. For females the corresponding figure was, by contrast, only 7.1 per cent.

Table 3.1
Cumulative per cent of the population born in 1953, 1958 and 1963 who were convicted, by age at first conviction

Age at first conviction	Males 1953	1958	1963	Females 1953	1958	1963
8	*	–	–	*	–	–
9	0.4	*	–	*	–	–
10	1.3	0.7	0.3	0.1	0.1	*
11	2.2	1.7	1.0	0.1	0.2	0.1
12	3.7	3.0	2.1	0.3	0.3	0.3
13	5.7	5.0	3.7	0.6	0.6	0.6
14	8.4	7.5	6.4	1.0	1.0	1.2
15	10.9	10.9	9.5	1.5	1.6	1.7
16	13.4	14.0	12.7	1.9	2.1	2.3
17	16.6	17.2	16.5	2.6	2.9	3.1
18	19.4	20.1	20.1	3.1	3.5	3.8
19	21.5	22.5	23.2	3.5	4.2	4.5
20	23.3	24.5	25.4	3.9	4.7	5.2
21	24.8	26.3	..	4.2	5.2	..
22	26.2	27.6	..	4.6	5.7	..
23	27.4	28.8	..	5.0	6.0	..
24	28.4	30.0	..	5.3	6.4	..
25	29.2	30.9	..	5.7	6.7	..
26	30.0	..	..	6.0	..	..
27	30.7	..	..	6.3	..	..
28	31.3	..	..	6.6	..	..
29	32.0	..	..	6.8	..	..
30	32.6	..	..	7.1	..	..

* Less than .05 per cent.
Source: Home Office, 1989b

Comparing the three cohorts up to age 15 it appears that participation in offending declines for later cohorts. But this is probably due to the increase in police cautioning which started in the late 1960s and accelerated during the 1970's, the time at which the two later cohorts were reaching the age of criminal responsibility. (Police cautions are not recorded in the Offenders Index – only convictions at court.) At age 18 and thereafter participation is higher among members of the later cohorts. There appears to have been an increase in female participation, as measured by convictions, despite the increase in cautioning, and this is evident from age 15 onwards. A greater proportion of females in later cohorts were convicted of a standard list offence.

Figure 3.1

Cumulative per cent of population born in 1953, 1958 and 1963 who were convicted, by age at first conviction.

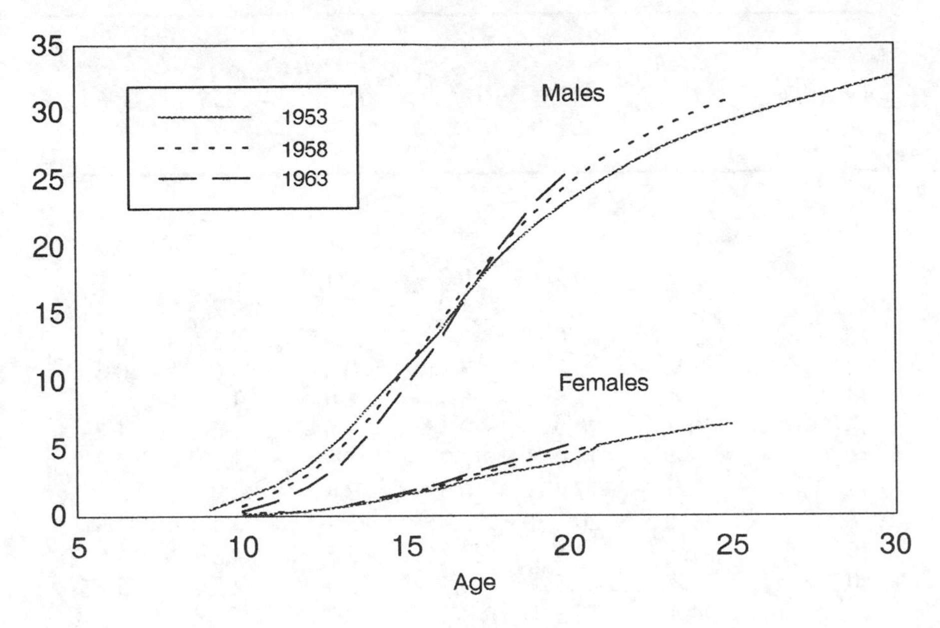

It can be shown that the ratio of male to female participation rates at any age is consistent with the ratios of male to female offending given in the previous chapter (see Table 2.3). Furthermore, a decline in the ratio over time, evident in Table 2.1, is also reflected in the decline in the ratio of participation rates. For example, at age 20 the ratio of male to female participation rates for the 1953 cohort is 6.0. (The 1953 cohort was aged 20 in 1973.) The male to female participation ratio at age 20 for the 1958 cohort is 5.2 (the 1958 cohort was aged 20 in 1978) and for the 1963 cohort at age 20 (in 1983) the ratio had declined to 4.9. Thus the greater increase in female offending referred to in Chapter 2 (which has led to a decline in the ratio between males and females) is, to a large extent, due to greater participation by females.

Table 3.1 also provides information on when offenders begin their criminal careers. For males about 17 per cent of each cohort had been convicted before age 18. This had risen to 23–25 per cent (depending on the cohort) by age 21. Thus most male offenders begin their careers as juveniles and young adults, and it can be seen from Figure 3.1 that the steepest increases are for the teenage years. (It was stated in the previous chapter that the peak age of offending is during the teenage years.) However, a not insignificant proportion of offenders start their career relatively late in life. For the 1953 cohort, which has been followed up for more years, about 7 per cent of the cohort, or nearly a quarter of offenders, did not start their career until after their 21st birthday. The pattern for females is quite similar except that the proportion of the cohorts participating in crime at any age is much lower.

Other studies have addressed the issue of participation of offending. One study (see Douglas *et. al.* 1968 and Wadsworth, 1979) is of particular interest because it provides information on a national cohort from an earlier generation: 5,011 persons born in one week in March 1946. In this group (after reweighting the sample accordingly) 14.6 per cent of males and 2.0 per cent of females were estimated to have been convicted or cautioned by the police for an indictable offence by age 17 and these proportions had risen to 17.9 and 2.5 by age 21. The rates for juveniles are comparable with those obtained for the later Research and Statistics Department cohorts mentioned above (although these did not include police cautions) but are a good deal lower for 21 year olds.

In addition, there have been three other longitudinal studies of cohorts drawn from more restricted geographical areas; two in London (Farrington, 1983 and 1989, and Ouston, 1984) and one in Newcastle (Miller *et. al.*, 1974), which provide information on participation[3.1]. In the first London sample, of 411 males born in 1953–1954 (the Cambridge Study of Delinquent Development), 25.7 per cent were convicted by age 18, 31.9 per cent by 21, 33.9 per cent by 25 and 37 per cent by age 32. The second London sample comprised 2,352 males and females born in 1959–60. When the group was 17 years of age 29.0 per cent of the males and 6.0 per cent of females had been cautioned by the police or convicted at court. The third local cohort was made up of 763 children born in Newcastle in 1947. By the time they were 19, 28.0 per cent of the males and 5.6 per cent of the females had been convicted. Results from these three local studies produce estimates of participation greater than the national samples of similar generations. This is probably due to the urban settings of these studies and the higher risk groups sampled. (The Cambridge Study of Delinquent Development selected males residing in a working class area of London).

Life table approach

Using data for 1965 and 1977 first McClintock and Avison (1968) and then Farrington (1981) were able to adopt a second method to estimate cumulative participation [3.2]. For all convicted offenders in 1965 and for a sample of 9,000 convicted in 1977 data were available showing the proportion of offenders at each age who were convicted for the first time. From knowledge of the number of people in the population at each age it was possible to estimate participation. The results are displayed in Table 3.2.

Table 3.2
Life table estimates of the cumulative per cent of the population who were convicted, by sex: 1965 and 1977

Participation up to age	*Males 1965*	*1977*	*Females 1965*	*1977*
17	10.8	11.7	2.0	2.1
21	16.7	21.8	3.0	4.7
25	20.4	26.6	3.6	6.2
30	23.6	30.3	4.3	7.9
40	27.3	35.8	5.5	10.6
50	29.4	39.4	6.5	12.3
Over 50	31.3	43.6	7.9	14.7

It can be seen that participation in offending increased substantially for each age for both males and females between 1965 and 1977. Interestingly, little increase seems to have occurred for juveniles (up to 17) compared with the larger increases for young adults (17 up to 21). The relatively small increases for juveniles may be due to the greater use of cautioning which took place from the late 1960s onwards; that is between the dates of these two studies.

The main advantage of the life table approach is that estimates of participation rates for older age groups can be calculated without having to wait for a birth cohort to reach that age. McClintock and Avison found on the basis of 1965 data 31.3 per cent of males and 7.9 per cent of females could expect to be convicted at some point in their lives. Farrington found that by 1977 this had risen to 43.6 per cent for males and 14.7 per cent for females. The difficulty with these estimates is that they do not relate to a particular generation so cannot be compared directly with estimates from the national cohort studies described previously.

Participation rates including police cautions

It was mentioned earlier that the substantial increase in police cautioning has probably affected comparisons of successive generations. The extent to which this may be true can be gauged from a study undertaken by Greater Manchester Police. This study examined the number of cautions and convictions at court awarded to 5,000 juveniles born in 1963 who came to the attention of the Greater Manchester Police. The sample included both males and females but the sex of the offender was not recorded. The data, which were kindly made available in the course of a project examining police cautioning (Laycock and Tarling, 1985), are set out in full in Appendix 2.

From Table A2 it can be seen that 2,271 males and females were cautioned only once while juveniles (up to their 17th birthday) but were not prosecuted and a further 64 were cautioned on two occasions but were not prosecuted. Thus of the entire sample of 5,000 offenders 2,335 or 47 per cent were dealt with by the police by way of caution but were not convicted at court. Of course it is not known how many of the offenders who were cautioned but not convicted as juveniles have since been convicted as adults. Nevertheless, comparing these results with the third Research and Statistics Department cohort, also born in 1963, strongly suggests that participation rates based on convictions alone are gross underestimates. Juvenile participation rates may be half as much again if cautions are included.

There is an alternative method of gauging the effects of police cautions on participation rates. Persons born in 1963 were 10 years old in 1973, 11 in 1974, 12 in 1975, 13 in 1976, 14 in 1977, 15 in 1978 and 16 in 1979. *Criminal Statistics* presents the number of males and females cautioned at each of these ages in each of these years. By this method it can be found that males born in 1963 amassed approximately 67,700 cautions when juveniles. It is also known that this cohort contained approximately 412,000 males. Data obtained for the 1963 Research and Statistics Department cohort indicated that 12.2 per cent were convicted as juveniles. Thus it can be estimated that approximately 50,250 males born in 1963 were convicted as juveniles. From the Greater Manchester data 1,427, or 28.5 per cent, were convicted as juveniles but were not cautioned, or, 71.5 per cent of those convicted had received at least one caution as well. Unfortunately it is not possible to separate males from females in the Greater Manchester Police data, but if it is assumed that the rates apply equally to both males and females it can be estimated that 50,250 x 71.5 per cent or 35,900 males had a previous caution. 67,700 - 35,900 = 31,800 males were cautioned but not convicted. Nearly 3 per cent had two cautions. This means that about 30,900 males were cautioned but not convicted. The estimated total number of males dealt with is equal to 50,250 + 30,900 = 81,150 and the participation rate would rise to 81,150/412,000 or 19.7 per cent.

However, Greater Manchester Police are less likely to caution juveniles than many other forces. If instead it is assumed that all of the males who were convicted had received one previous caution, then approximately 17,400 males were cautioned but not convicted and the participation rate including cautions would rise to 67,700/412,000 or 16.4 per cent. In practice the true estimate of the participation rate is likely to be somewhere in between 19.7 and 16.4 per cent. But both are higher than the 12.2 per cent obtained from convictions alone.

A similar approach can be applied to females. Those born in 1963 (approximately 392,000) amassed 21,600 cautions as juveniles. If the same assumptions are made, namely; first, that 71.5 per cent those convicted had one previous caution and second, that all those convicted had one previous caution the participation rate would be between 6.3 and 5.5 per cent; more than twice the rate if only convictions are included (2.3 per cent) [3.3].

The conclusions from this body of research are that participation in offending as indicated by those convicted for indictable, standard list or a broadly similar group of offences is high, perhaps surprisingly so. It is higher still in inner city or urban areas. The time does not seem to be far off when 50 per cent of the male population can expect a conviction for such an offence at some point in their life. Participation in offending has been increasing since the war if police cautions are taken into account. However, the extent of this increase cannot be measured with any certainty as no recent national cohort has included information on cautions.

Participation by type of offence

Table 3.3 shows the proportion of the three cohorts who had at some stage been convicted of each of the main types of offence. In order to compare across generations participation is up to age 20. Obviously an offender could have been convicted of more than one type of offence during his or her career and hence could be included in more than one offence category.

Table 3.3
Per cent of the population born in 1953, 1958 and 1963 convicted before age 21, by type of offence

Type of offence	*Males*			*Females*		
	1953	*1958*	*1963*	*1953*	*1958*	*1963*
Violence against the person	2.9	4.4	5.0	0.2	0.4	0.6
Burglary	8.3	9.1	6.4	0.4	0.5	0.6
Robbery	0.4	0.6	0.6	*	*	*
Sexual offences	0.6	0.6	0.5	–	*	*
Theft from shops	2.7	3.2	4.0	1.7	2.1	2.5
Theft of motor vehicle	6.2	6.9	6.2	0.2	0.3	0.3
Other theft and handling stolen goods	12.9	11.9	12.0	1.7	1.8	2.0
Criminal damage	4.3	6.8	6.9	0.1	0.4	0.4
Fraud	1.5	1.8	2.0	0.4	0.5	0.7
Drugs offences	0.6	0.7	1.1	0.1	0.1	0.2
Other indictable offences	0.4	0.6	1.3	*	0.1	0.3
Other summary offences	3.0	3.5	1.9	0.2	0.3	0.2

*Less than 0.05 per cent
Source: Home Office, 1989b

Considering males first, it can be seen that participation rates were highest for some property offences; other theft and handling stolen goods, criminal damage, burglary, theft of motor vehicles and shoplifting. Participation in violence was comparable to some categories of property crimes but rates were much lower for robbery, sexual offences and drug offences.

Contrasting participation rates for different cohorts reveals some interesting patterns. Participation in offences of violence, in particular, has been increasing significantly (from 2.9 to 5.0) as has participation in shoplifting and drug offences, although these increases have been less dramatic. However, participation in burglary has fallen substantially (from 8.3 to 6.4).

For females the highest participation rates were for shoplifting and other theft and handling. The proportions convicted for all other offences were much lower. Participation rates for shoplifting and also for violence have increased over time but rates have remained fairly constant for the other offence types.

Self-reported offending

The growing number of self-report studies show that offending, or at least petty offending, is much more widespread than official records would suggest. Self-reports are invariably confined to less serious offences: minor violence and burglary being the most serious. They also indicate that the difference between male and female participation rates is often less than suggested by official statistics.

Many self-report studies have asked juveniles, particularly males, about their involvement in delinquent acts. For example, a large number of the 584 boys aged between 11–15 in Gladstone's (1978) study admitted committing acts of vandalism; 65 per cent or more had 'scratched desk at school', 'broken a bottle in the street' or 'broken a window in an empty house'. Lower rates (20 per cent or less) were found for more serious acts such as, 'damaged a telephone kiosk' or 'slashed train seats'.

Belson (1975) found that all the 1,425 London boys aged between 13 and 16 that he interviewed admitted to some form of stealing: 88 per cent had at some time stolen something from school, 70 per cent from a shop, 18 per cent from a telephone box, 25 per cent from a motor vehicle, 5 per cent had taken a motor vehicle.

Shapland (1978), too, found high rates for shoplifting and vandalism, although her study was confined to only 51 boys.

Three studies, Jamison (1977), Mawby (1980) and Riley and Shaw (1985) interviewed samples of girls as well as boys and can thus provide comparisons between the sexes. Some results from these studies are shown in Table 3.4.

The results in Table 3.4 are fairly typical, confirming the higher participation rates obtained from self-report studies and, in many cases, smaller differences in participation rates between males and females than recorded by official statistics. Nevertheless, the differences between males and females shows a similar pattern, although less pronounced, in that the proportion of males and females who admit committing less serious offences (theft or not paying the correct fare, for example) are similar but males are more likely to commit more serious offences, such as offences of burglary and violence.

The evidence on self-reported offending so far presented has been obtained from juveniles or teenagers, but the self-report data collected by the two British Crime Surveys provide information for older age groups. Respondents in both the 1982 and 1984 British Crime Surveys were asked whether they had committed a range of offences. The number of offences that respondents were asked about was much greater in 1982 than in 1984. Mayhew and Elliott (1990) compared, where possible, results obtained from both surveys and found that admissions were generally twice as high in 1984 than in 1982, which, they point out, is probably due to changes in the format of the 1984 self-report questions.

Table 3.5 presents data on the seven offences included in the 1984 BCS and on one offence ('involved in a fight') from the 1982 BCS.

Table 3.4
Self–reported offending by sex: per cent having admitted committing the offences within the last 12 months.

Offence	*Jamison (1977)*		*Mawby (1980)*		*Riley & Shaw (1985)*	
	Boys	*Girls*	*Boys*	*Girls*	*Boys*	*Girls*
Shoplifting	47	22	54	39	47	22
Theft from school	53	47	42	44	–	–
House breaking	12	1	6	1	–	–
Burglary (other than house)	–	–	12	1	–	–
Breaking into empty building	–	–	37	8	–	–
Robbery by threat	–	–	25	12	7	5
Violence using a weapon	21	10	19	8	–	–
Carried a weapon (eg knife) intending to use it on someone if necessary	27	10	–	–	47	17
Travelled on a bus or train without a ticket or deliber–ately paid the wrong fare	60	60	76	59	74	67

Jamison (1977): 781 boys and 501 girls from three different areas in Southern England. Mawby (1980): 327 boys and 264 girls aged 13–15 in one school in Sheffield. Riley and Shaw (1985): nationally representative sample of 378 boys and 373 girls aged 14 and 15.

Table 3.5
British Crime Survey 1984: percentage of respondents admitting to having committed the offence once or more in the past year, by age and sex

Males		*Age*		
Offence	*16–21*	*22–30*	*31–40*	*41 and over*
Involved in a fight [1]	28	10	6	2
Stealing office supplies	32	41	39	18
Pilfering from work	9	12	10	4
Fiddling work expenses	13	17	14	5
Evading proper fares	29	15	6	2
Evading customs duties	11	19	18	12
Tax evasion	4	8	8	4
Smoking cannabis	13	10	4	1

Females		*Age*		
Offence	*16–21*	*22–30*	*31–40*	*41 and over*
Involved in a fight [1]	5	1	1	*
Stealing office supplies	26	30	24	10
Pilfering from work	*	1	1	1
Fiddling work expenses	2	6	4	1
Evading proper fares	24	10	6	2
Evading customs duties	9	13	15	7
Tax evasions	1	2	2	1
Smoking cannabis	6	6	2	*

* less than .5
1 1982 BCS
Source: 1982 and 1984 British Crime Survey; weighted data.

Despite the question over the absolute validity of these data they do broadly confirm the now familiar pattern. Offending declines with age; the percentage admitting having committed the offence is lowest for those persons aged 41 and over. However, it can be seen that in many cases (stealing or pilfering from work, fiddling expenses and evading tax or customs duties) higher rates were found among persons in their twenties and thirties than among young adults. This may be because the opportunities to commit these crimes are more restricted for young adults. Nevertheless, the results do at least suggest that the peak age and the mean age of offending for some specific types of crime may be higher than that revealed by statistics of persons cautioned or prosecuted at court. (In Chapter 2 it was shown that, with the exception of sexual offences, the peak age and mean age of offending were highest for offences of fraud and forgery). Males were more likely to have committed the offence than females and the ratio between the sexes is lower for less serious crimes or crimes where each sex had a similar opportunity to commit them; stealing office supplies, evading proper fares, evading customs duties and smoking cannabis. In contrast violence (involved in a fight) was an offence committed predominantly by young males.

Further confirmation of this pattern is provided by the Cambridge Study of Delinquent Development. The entire cohort of 411 males was interviewed at ages 14, 18–19 and 32 (a subset was also interviewed at 21 and 25) about the offences they had committed during a few years prior to the interview. Thus this study provides evidence of offending at different ages but rather than being cross-sectional (different people of different ages at one point in time) it assembled information on offending for the same people at different points in time, that is, at different ages. Farrington (1989a) reports the result which are summarised below.

Table 3.6
Proportion of the Cambridge Study of Delinquent Development London cohort who admitted committing an offence at certain periods in their life

Offence	*Between Ages*			
	10 – 14	*15 – 18*	*26 – 32*	*10 – 32**
Burglary	13.2	10.9	2.2	22
Shoplifting	39.3	15.5	5.5	48
Theft of vehicle	7.5	15.2	3.0	23
Theft from vehicle	9.3	13.4	2.3	22
Theft from machine	14.7	19.1	1.7	30
Theft from work	2.3	**	23.9	32
Assault	39.8	45.2	36.1	70
Vandalism	71.1	21.2	1.1	74
Drug Use	0.3	31.5	19.9	38
Fraud	73.4	**	52.8	8

* Estimates (see Farrington, 1989a for details of estimating procedures
** Not asked

Broadly Table 3.6 shows that burglary, shoplifting, theft of and from vehicles, theft from slot machines and vandalism all declined substantially with age. The most noticeable was vandalism; 71 per cent admitted committing this offence at some time between age 10 and 14 but only 1 per cent between age 26 and 32. In contrast, theft from work, assault, drug use and fraud did not decline and in some cases increased with age. The last column shows cumulative participation; the proportion who had ever admitted committing the offence at any of the five interviews. It is comparatively high for most types of offence; 70 per cent or more admitted committing assault or vandalism and approximately 50 per cent admitted shoplifting.

Mott (1985) presents further analysis of the 1982 British Crime Survey data (for both England and Wales and Scotland) on the use of cannabis. There was a tendency (though not statistically significant) for more of both sexes aged between 16 and 24 in the Scottish rather than in the England and Wales sample, to say they had used cannabis at some time and had used it at least once during the last year. This was particularly true of those still in education and those who had completed their full-time education aged 17 and older.

Riley (1984 and 1985) examined the 1982 and 1984 British Crime Survey self-report data on drink driving. Overall about one in five males (22 per cent) and one in eleven females (9 per cent) admitted having recently driven when they 'knew' they were over the legal limit. For both sexes there was a significant age effect; males and females between the ages of 16 and 30 were much more likely to drink and drive than those aged 31 to 60 and few drivers 61 and over admitted drinking and driving.

Comparison of official records and self-reported offending

Several studies have attempted to compare individuals' self-reported offending with their official records of offending and have always found a close, but by no means perfect, correspondence between the two sources. For example, Shapland (1978) and Mawby (1980) asked their subjects whether or not they had come into contact with the police and/or been convicted of the offences they admitted. Unfortunately however, in neither study were these answers confirmed by reference to official records.

West and Farrington (1977) and Farrington (1989a), on the other hand, did compare self-report information with official records and their study is important for this reason. First, they were able to confirm that members of their cohort had answered correctly about their contacts with the police, thus providing further confidence that people are prepared to give truthful answers in such studies. The proportion of those who denied committing the offence of a particular type at any time but who were in fact convicted of such an offence was less than 4 per cent.

Another general finding was that offenders who admitted committing many offences were more likely to have been convicted and offenders committing more serious offences were also more likely to be caught and convicted at some stage in their career. More than half of those who committed burglary or theft of a vehicle received a conviction for these offences. This dropped to about a quarter for theft from vehicles and further to one in eight for those who committed shoplifting or assault. Low percentages were found for theft from machines, theft from work, drug use (all at 7 per cent), vandalism (6 per cent) and fraud (3 per cent).

The results of these, and other comparisons made by Farrington (1989a), led him to conclude that official records and self-reported offending were measuring the same underlying concepts but with different measurement biases. Furthermore, he suggests they are comparable and complementary measures and both are valuable in advancing knowledge about delinquency and crime.

Participation rates in other countries

Visher and Roth (1986) were commissioned by the Panel on Research on Criminal Careers to review the research evidence on participation in offending, and they presented results from many studies carried out in the U.S. together with results from the British studies described earlier. Since their report was published further information has come to light for Germany, New Zealand and Sweden. The purpose here is not to reproduce details of all the studies that they reviewed but, more modestly, to present some information from other countries in order to place the British results in context. In fact most of the U.S. studies are not comparable with their British counterparts as they included a broader range of offences such as status offences (for example truancy) and minor infractions that brought the subjects to the attention of the police or the courts. Furthermore, many comprised only certain small sub-groups of the population. Because information on juvenile offending is kept separately from information on adult offending in most U.S. jurisdictions (so it is not possible to readily obtain for adults information on the crimes they committed as juveniles) the majority of studies conducted there were confined to juveniles and participation is reported up to age 18.

The most directly comparable U.S. data comes from the two Philadelphia birth cohorts analysed by Wolfgang and his colleagues (Wolfgang *et. al.* 1972 and Tracy *et. al.* 1990). The first Philadelphia birth cohort comprised 9,945 males born in 1945 and resident in Philadelphia. By their 18th birthday 13.6 per cent had been arrested by the police for an index offence. (Index offences - homicide, rape, robbery, aggravated assault, burglary, larcency and auto theft - are the nearest equivalent to standard list offences although index offences are somewhat narrower in coverage and exclude some of the less serious offences included in the standard list)[3.4]. The rate of 13.6 per cent is not dissimilar to the 16.6 per cent recorded for the 1953 Research and Statistics Department cohort (see Table 3.1) bearing in mind the more limited offence coverage. The second Philadelphia birth cohort was much larger and included females as well as males. It comprised 28,338 males and females born in 1958 and resident in Philadelphia. By the age of 18, 17.9 per cent of the males had been arrested for an index offence which compares with 17.2 per cent for the 1958 Research and Statistics Department cohort at the same age (see Table 3.1). For the females in the Philadelphia cohort 4.0 per cent had been arrested for index offences, compared with 2.9 per cent for the females in the 1958 Research and Statistics Department cohort (see Table 3.1).

Donnell and Lovell (1982) report results of offending for a representative cohort of 8,801 New Zealand males born in 1957. All members of the cohort were followed up while juveniles; in New Zealand this is up to age 17. Both offences resulting in conviction at court and police warnings (broadly equivalent to police cautions in Britain) were included. The exact offence coverage is not clear in the report although from the description it appears to exclude non-criminal acts such as truancy or 'neglect' but may well include more minor offences not included in the standard list. Nevertheless, by age 17, 20.1 per cent of the cohort had come to official notice (conviction at court or police warning). This compares with 14.0 per cent by age 17 for the 1958 Research and Statistics Department cohort (see Table 3.1). The reason for the higher rate in New Zealand is probably due to the inclusion of police warnings and the slightly broader category of offences.

Information is available for Scandinavia. 'Project Metropolitan' followed up a cohort of 15,117 males and females born in the Stockholm Metropolitan Area in 1953 (Wikstrom, 1987). The offences included seem broadly similar to standard list offences in that they include offences of violence and against property, drug offences, major traffic offences (but not minor ones such as speeding) and a few other crimes. The cohort was followed up to age 25 or 26 by which time 31 per cent of the males and 6 per cent of the females were 'registered' for a criminal offence. Similarly a second study (Stattin, *et. al*., 1989) followed up nearly 1,400 persons born in 1955 and living in another large town (not identified) in Sweden. Approximately half the cohort were males and half females. The proportion 'registered' by age 30 was very similar, 32.5 per cent of males and 7.2 per cent of females. A 'Project Metropolitan' was also undertaken in Copenhagen, Denmark. Approximately 11,500 boys born in that city in 1953 were followed up until age 23 by which time 21 per cent had been registered for a non-traffic offence[3.5]. The results from all three Scandinavian studies are very similar to those of the Research and Statistics Department cohorts at comparable ages (see Table 3.1).

Analyses of birth cohorts has recently begun in Germany where boys and girls from one state (Baden–Wurttemberg) have been followed up. Results for the oldest cohort, those born in 1970, reveal that 13 per cent of males and 5 per cent of females had 'police records' by age 17. Unfortunately no details are given of the type of offences committed but the figures are not too dissimilar to those found in this country although the female participation rate in Germany seems higher.

International comparisons are always hazardous; definitions (convictions, police cautions or arrests) coverage and data sources (court or police records) are never quite the same. Nevertheless, one conclusion is clear; the high, perhaps surprisingly high, fraction of the general population that engage in crime at some time in their life in this country is matched closely in other countries too.

4 FREQUENCY OF OFFENDING AND LENGTH OF CRIMINAL CAREERS

The last chapter considered participation in offending, that is the proportion of people who commit an offence up to a certain age. It was shown there that most offenders commit one or only a few offences before ending their criminal careers, whereas others commit many offences frequently over a prolonged period. It is important to know what proportion falls into different groups if we are trying to conceptualise the kind of offenders we have to deal with. Frequency or rate of offending, and the length of criminal careers are considered in this Chapter.

Frequency of offending

All studies of offenders, whether birth cohorts followed up over time or cross-sectional samples of offenders appearing at court or in prison, show that the number of crimes committed varies between offenders but before presenting results it is essential to clarify some terminology.

The number of convictions (or previous convictions) is often used as a measure of criminal history or of the frequency with which offenders commit crime. Leaving aside the problem (discussed in Chapter 1) that not all crimes committed by offenders lead to conviction a further problem arises over the distinction between convictions and court appearances. Most researchers cite previous convictions when in fact they record previous court appearances – the number of occasions in the past that an offender has appeared at court and been convicted of at least one offence. But at any one court appearance an offender may be convicted of more than one offence; if several crimes are committed in quick succession it is common practice for the offender to be dealt with and convicted of all of them at the same court hearing. Thus recording previous court appearances (even if called previous convictions) may actually understate the number of known previous offences committed by that offender.

On the other hand, recording the actual number of convictions is not entirely without problems as a measure of the number of offences an offender has committed. It is also not uncommon for one offence or incident to result in several charges and convictions. An example might be unauthorised taking of a motor vehicle which can be seen as one incident or offence but may well lead to several convictions – unauthorised taking, no insurance, no driving licence, driving while disqualified etc. Another example might be rape. In addition to the conviction for rape if the attack involved violence there may well be other convictions for actual or grievous bodily harm. Offences of dishonesty, particularly fraud, are notoriously difficult too. If a person steals a credit card and then uses it in quick succession to obtain goods from five different shops is that six crimes (five purchases plus the theft of the card) or one crime? If the perpetrator is caught it is likely to result in six charges and convictions but only one court appearance.

While neither conviction nor court appearances is a perfect measure of known offending it is essential to be aware of the distinction between the two when interpreting the results of various studies, particularly when using the data to estimate rates of offending. Throughout this chapter the measure used will be clearly stated.

Both convictions and court appearances were recorded for the 1953 cohort and from these data it was found that the male offenders amassed nearly 32,500 convictions but only 23,300 court appearances. Thus the ratio of convictions to court appearances is 1.4:1 and this can be used where necessary as a weighting or conversion factor when estimating one from the other. (The ratio for females is virtually the same, 1.3:1.)

Table 4.1 presents information on the criminal histories of three separate samples of male offenders: the male offenders in the 1953 cohort, the sample of male offenders convicted at the Crown Court and the sample of male prisoners released on parole. These data sets were described in Chapter 1.

It can be seen that for the male *offenders* in the 1953 cohort 45.1 per cent had received only 1 conviction, 18.2 per cent 2 convictions and so on. The percentage declines as the number of convictions increases such that only 0.7 per cent had 12 convictions. The proportion with 13, 14, 15 etc convictions was similarly small but as the distribution has a long 'tail' the proportion with 13 or more appears relatively high at 6.4 per cent. Similar distributions occurred for the sample of offenders convicted at the Crown Court and for the sample of parolees. However, the distribution is less skewed, or more evenly distributed, for the Crown Court sample and even more so for the sample of parolees. This simply reflects the fact that offenders sentenced at the Crown Court are more serious offenders, in terms of previous involvement in crime, than offenders generally and prisoners or parolees are yet more likely to have longer criminal records. Nevertheless, the pattern is typical, with some offenders having few convictions while others have many.

Table 4.1
Per cent of male offenders with k convictions or court appearances

Number convictions or court appearances k	*1953 Cohort (convictions)*	*Offenders sentenced at the Crown Court (court appearances)*	*Prisoners released on parole (court appearances)*
	per cent	*per cent*	*per cent*
1	45.1	21.6	9.5
2	18.2	10.0	7.9
3	8.7	9.6	11.0
4	5.7	7.9	8.8
5	3.9	7.0	8.0
6	3.2	6.4	6.1
7	2.6	5.6	7.5
8	1.7	5.0	6.1
9	1.7	4.6	4.7
10	1.1	3.7	4.6
11	1.0	3.8	3.4
12	0.7	3.2	4.7
13 or more	6.4	11.7	17.8
Number of offenders	8601	1851	738

Females were not included in the sample of parolees but information on female offenders in the 1953 cohort and in the Crown Court study are shown in Table 4.2.

Table 4.2
Per cent of female offenders with k convictions or court appearances

Number of convictions or court appearances k	*1953 cohort (convictions) per cent*	*Offenders sentenced at the Crown Court (court appearances) per cent*
1	64.3	46.5
2	18.1	12.8
3	6.4	10.6
4	4.2	10.2
5	2.3	4.0
6	1.2	4.0
7	1.0	2.7
8	0.3	2.2
9	0.1	1.8
10 or more	2.0	5.3
Number of offenders	1803	226

A similar pattern emerges for females; a large per cent of offenders having few convictions with a decreasing proportion having many convictions. Contrasting the results in Tables 4.1 and 4.2 it is noticeable that the distribution for females is even more skewed; a higher proportion having one conviction or one court appearance than males. Thus female offenders generally have less extensive criminal records than their male counterparts.

Percentage of convictions attributable to offenders with k convictions

An alternative way of viewing these data is to consider the percentage of all the convictions amassed by a cohort that are attributable to those with 1 conviction, 2 convictions etc[(4.1)].

This approach was first adopted by Wolfgang *et. al*. (1972) in their famous Philadelphia birth cohort study. In their study 9,945 boys born in Philadelphia in 1945 were followed up to age 18. Between them, the cohort amassed 10,214 arrests but 52 per cent of these arrests had involved only 6.3 per cent of the boys – the 6.3 per cent comprising those who had 5 or more arrests – whom the authors called the 'chronic offenders'. This result, that few members of a cohort account for a large number of crimes, which Blumstein *et. al*. (1985) described as a 'tantalising finding', has attracted a good deal of attention and comment. Clearly if the small group of chronic offenders could be identified early in their criminal careers and targetted for some form of successful intervention to reduce their offending this could have a significant impact on crime.

Since the Wolfgang *et. al*. study, other cohort studies have found broadly similar results. The Cambridge Study of Delinquent Development which followed up a cohort of approximately 400 males in London, found that about 6 per cent (those with 6 or more convictions) accounted for about half the convictions amassed by the cohort.

The Home Office Research and Statistics Department cohorts provide further evidence of this phenomenon. For example, about 7 per cent of males in the 1953 cohort (those who had been convicted of 6 or more offences) accounted for 65 per cent of the convictions amassed by the cohort. These are similarly tantalising findings.

To date little work has been undertaken on cohorts of females, the exception being the Home Office Research and Statistics Department cohorts. The 1953 cohort suggests that the chronic female offenders (those with 6 or more convictions) comprised only 0.5 per cent of the cohort and accounted for about 29 per cent of all convictions amassed by the cohort. Fewer females commit crimes leading to conviction and a greater proportion of those who do, compared with males, are convicted on only 1 or 2 occasions. If the definition of a chronic female offender is reduced to those with 3 or more convictions then 1.6 per cent of the 1953 cohort would be defined as chronic offenders and they account for about 58 per cent of all convictions.

Returning to the males the tantalising finding turns out, on closer inspection, not to be so attractive nor to present the potential opportunities for crime control which it suggests at first sight. It was shown in the previous chapter that about one third of the males in the 1953 cohort were convicted at least once, but this means that approximately two–thirds were not convicted. Thus it is more appropriate to consider the chronic offenders as a proportion of *offenders*, those with at least one conviction, rather than as a proportion of the entire cohort which includes the majority without a conviction. On this basis, the chronics represent about 18 per cent of offenders (see Table 4.1) compared with 7 per cent of the entire cohort. Of course, 18 per cent accounting for 65 per cent of convictions is still an important disproportionality but with much less impact than 7 per cent.

A similar result is obtained for females. A shift to a more appropriate denominator indicates that females with 3 or more convictions represent about 18 per cent of *offenders* (see Table 4.2) accounting for 58 per cent of the convictions.

Age of onset and frequency of offending

Many studies have found that the age at which a criminal begins his or her career (age of onset) is related to the number of subsequent convictions in that the earlier a person begins his/her criminal career the more convictions he/she is likely to obtain (see Blumstein *et. al.*, 1986). This relationship was found to be the case for offenders in the 1953 cohort. For males there was a clear relationship; the average number of convictions declining with age of onset. To some extent this result can be anticipated as the earlier a male begins his career the more time he has to commit further offences; obviously those who begin their careers in the mid-twenties have only 5 or 6 years to reoffend. (At the time of this study the cohort had only been followed up to age 31.) Nevertheless this reasoning is less compelling for juveniles, 15 year olds have 16 years to commit offences which is not much less time than 11 year olds (20 years) but the average number of convictions was found to be a good deal less. There is obviously a need to follow up cohorts for longer periods and into late adulthood, to see whether the nature of the relationship changes.

For females the pattern was not quite so clear, reflecting the fact that females generally commit fewer offences and tend to begin their careers later.

Modelling the probability of a further conviction

If any potential gains in terms of crime reduction are to be realised by targetting action on the chronic offenders they must be identified prospectively and at some early point in their criminal career. This too presents problems. Blumstein and Moitra (1980) were the first to point out that in any group of offenders, statistical chance alone would result in some committing more crimes than others even if all the members of the group had the *same* propensity to commit crime. In other words, to find retrospectively a sub-group of offenders who had committed a disproportionate number of crimes, or who had a disproportionate number of convictions, is, to some extent, nothing more than one would expect. The chronics may be no different from the non-chronics in their propensity to commit crime. To explore this issue further Blumstein and Moitra (1980) calculated for the members of the first Philadelphia birth cohort the probability that an offender who was arrested for the kth time would be arrested at least once more. The report of the Panel on Research on Criminal Careers (Blumstein *et. al*. 1986, p90) presented these probabilities together with probabilities from other cohorts, including the cohort of London males which form the Cambridge Study of Delinquent Development and other U.S. cohorts assembled by Shannon (1981). The data for the Philadelphia and London cohorts are reproduced in Table 4.3 together with data from the 1953 male and female cohorts.

Table 4.3
Probability of receiving a further arrest, conviction or court appearance after receiving k–l arrests, convictions or court appearances.

Number of arrests, convictions or court appearances	*Philadelphia Cohort (arrests)*	*London Cohort (court appearances)*	*1953 Cohort males (convictions)*	*1953 Cohort females (convictions)*
1	.35	.33	.33	.07
2	.54	.63	.55	.36
3	.65	.74	.67	.46
4	.72	.69	.76	.63
5	.72	.76	.80	.63
6	.74	.69	.83	.67
7	.79	.91	.83	.74
8	.77	.90	.83	.71
9	.80	.78	.87	.86
10	.83	.86	.85	.95
11	.79	–	.88	.75
12	.80	–	.88	.89
13	.73	–	.90	.83
14	.88	–	.87	.75
15	.70	–	.89	1.00

Considering the three cohorts of males (the first three columns of Table 4.3) a remarkably consistent pattern emerges. In all three the probability of getting one arrest, conviction or court appearance is about one third. This is simply the participation rate discussed in the previous chapter. Of those who have been arrested or convicted once, one half to two–thirds go on to receive a second. Of those arrested or convicted twice, between two–thirds to three quarters are arrested or convicted a third time. Thus up to this point the probability of a subsequent arrest or conviction rises but after about the third arrest the rearrest or reconviction probability levels off and remains persistently high thereafter[4.2]. This becomes clearer graphically and Figures 4.1 and 4.2 show these 'continuance' probabilities for the 1953 cohort; first for males and second for females.

Figure 4.1
Probability of receiving a further conviction: Males, 1953 cohort.

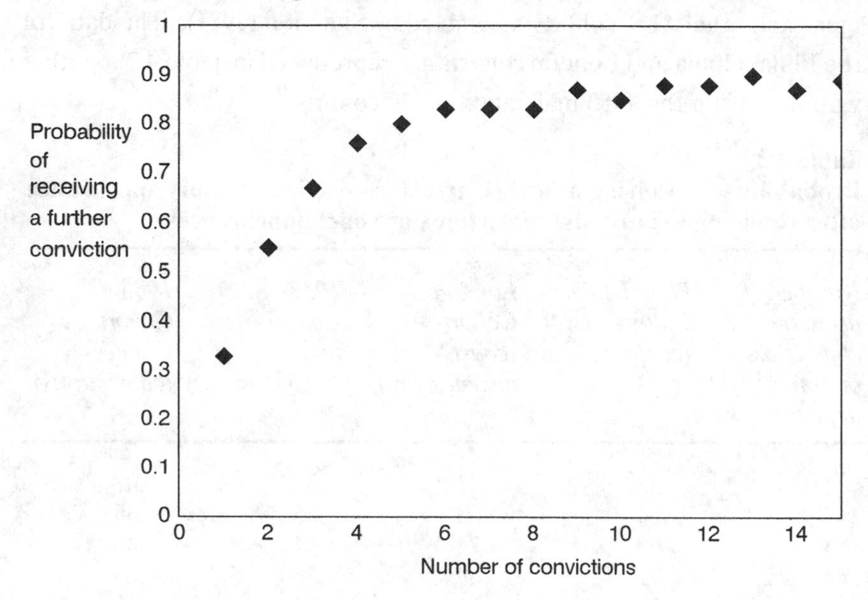

Figure 4.2
Probability of receiving a further conviction: Females, 1953 cohort

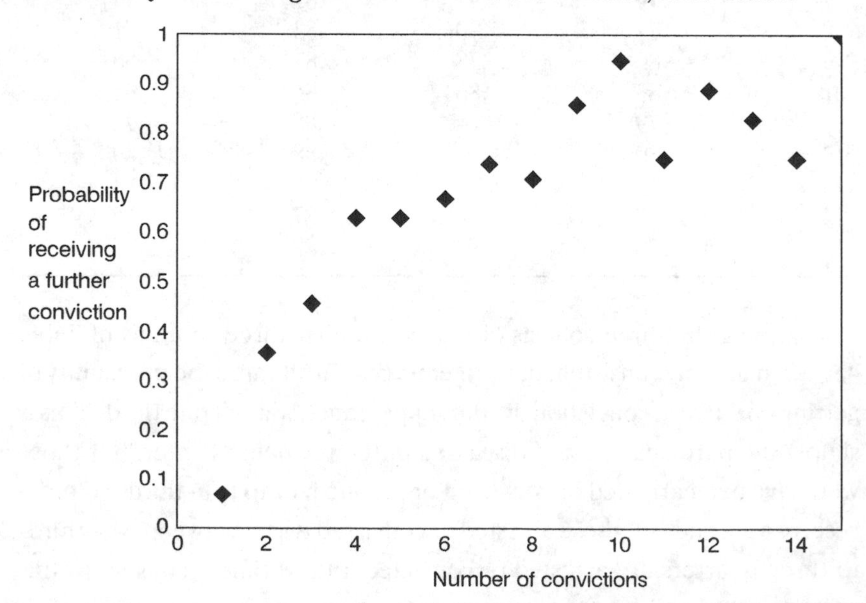

Blumstein and Moitra (1980) analysed the Philadelphia data and pointed out that after the third arrest the conditional probability of obtaining at least one more arrest was fairly constant, with an average value of .72, no matter how many arrests had already been recorded. They went on to test this assumption by fitting a 'shifted geometric distribution'. Their model is:-

$$\Pr[k \geq k-1] = p_1 p_2 p_3 \sum_{j=k}^{\infty} r^{j-3}(1-r) = p_1 p_2 p_3 r^{k-3}$$

They constrained p_1, p_2, p_3 to be equal to the values found in the data. Hence:-

$p_1 = .35$

$p_2 = .54$

$p_3 = .65$

$r = .72$

This model, with the above values, fitted the data well(4.3). The model is 'memoryless' in the sense that the probability of accummulating any number of additional arrests after the third is independent of the number already received. Furthermore, the expected number of future arrests at any stage after the third is r/(1–r), which is also independent of the number of arrests already recorded. With r = .72 the expected number of future arrests is 2.6. Thus knowing the number of previous arrests (for those who have had three or more) is no guide to identifying which offenders will go on to have many more arrests. A further result from their analysis is that the expected proportion of offenders who account for 50 per cent of the arrests is about 18 per cent, a figure in line with the actual findings. They showed, that this result is fairly insensitive to the value of r.

In a later paper, Blumstein *et. al.* (1985) extended their analysis of the Philadelphia cohort and replicated the analysis on the London cohort. Re-examining the Philadelphia data they found that a refinement to the model fitted the data better. Essentially they distinguished those with three, four and five arrests who had a probability of .72 of being arrested again from those who had six or more arrests who had an average probability of being re-arrested of .80. Thus the model was $p_1 = .35$, $p_2 = .54$, $p_3 = .65$, $p_4 = p_5 = p_6 = .72$, and $r = .8$. In addition to producing a better fit, the model estimates that the expected number of future arrests after any given arrest from the sixth onwards is r/(1–r) or .8/.2 which equals 4.

A similar analysis was carried out on the approximately 400 members of the London cohort. The geometric model that best fitted the data was $p_1 = .33$, $p_2 = .63$, $p_3 = p_4 = p_5 = p_6 = .72$ and $r = .87$.

Similar analysis was applied to the males and females in the 1953 birth cohort. This kind of analysis has not been undertaken before on a cohort of females. The probabilities of receiving a further conviction are shown in Table 4.3 and are presented graphically in Figures 4.1 and 4.2. The model that best fitted the data for males was found to be $p_1 = .33$, $p_2 = .55$, $p_3 = .67$, $p_4 = .76$, $p_5 = .80$, $p_6 = p_7 = p_8 = .83$, $r = .87$. This model produced a good fit, $\chi^2 = 6.2$ with 8 df. Thus the expected number of future convictions for those with 9 or more convictions is $.87/.13 = 6.7$.

An interesting pattern emerges for the females. It will be recalled that only 7 per cent of females in the cohort received at least one conviction compared with 33 per cent of males. Of those receiving one conviction 36 per cent went on to receive a second. This too is lower than that for males (55 per cent). The probability of a further conviction generally increases up to the 9th conviction but the probability is less than that for males with the same number of convictions. From the 9th onwards the probabilities vary somewhat which is due to the small number of females with 9 or more convictions even in a large birth cohort of just over 25,000. The best fitting model for females was found to be $p_1 = .07$, $p_2 = .36$, $p_3 = .46$, $p_4 = p_5 = p_6 = .64$, $p_7 = p_8 = .72$, $r = .86$. This model produced a good fit, $\chi^2 = 8.6$, with 9 df. Thus it can be seen that for the females with 8 convictions, albeit a small number, the probability of receiving a further conviction is .86, virtually identical to that for males (.87).

Thus all the above analyses reveal a similar pattern, an increasing probability of receiving a further arrest or conviction up to some threshold or plateau at which point the probability is high and consistent.

Length of criminal careers

In the previous section the extent of a criminal career was measured in terms of the number of convictions. The length of a criminal career can also be measured by the number of years between the first and last offence. From the evidence presented earlier, that many people commit few crimes and that much crime is committed by teenagers, it would appear that many criminal careers are very short. It is difficult to obtain precise estimates of the length of criminal careers as few cohorts have been followed up for a long period. However, data for the 1953 cohort provides some information, at least up to age 31. Offenders Index records the age of the offender at the time of each conviction and from this the length of each offender's criminal career could be estimated. The results of this analysis are presented in Table 4.4.

Table 4.4
Length of criminal careers: 1953 cohort males and females

Length of criminal careers (years)	*1953 cohort*	
	Males	*Females*
Less than 1 yr	57.6	79.7
1 < 2	4.1	4.0
2 < 3	3.6	3.4
3 < 4	3.3	1.8
4 < 5	3.3	1.6
5 < 6	3.0	1.1
6 < 7	2.7	1.2
7 < 8	2.5	1.3
8 < 9	2.4	1.1
9 < 10	2.7	0.8
10 < 11	2.1	0.9
11 < 12	1.8	0.9
12 < 13	2.3	0.4
13 < 14	1.9	0.4
14 < 15	1.5	0.3
15 or more	5.2	1.1
Average length of career (all offenders)	3.3 years	1.1 years
Average length of career offenders with more than 1 court appearance)	7.4 years	4.9 years
90th percentile (all offenders)	11.13 years	4.5 years
Maximum recorded career[1]	22 years	20 years

1 In 1953 the age of responsibility was 8 years and there were two males in the cohort who received their first conviction when 8 and a further conviction at age 30.

The results indeed confirm that the majority of careers are of short duration, nearly 60 per cent of male and 80 per cent of female careers being less than one year. Most of these offenders had only one conviction. The average length of a career depends on whether those with only one conviction or one court appearance are included or excluded. The length of their career is 0. Separate averages first including then excluding one time offenders were calculated and both are shown in Table 4.4.

The average length of a career for the entire group of male offenders was found to be 3.3 years. Omitting offenders with one court appearance, the average career length for the remainder rises to 7.4 years. Ninety per cent of all males had a career of less than 12 – 13 years. Female careers were much shorter, the average career length being 1.1 years rising to 4.9 years when one time offenders are excluded. All estimates in the table must be regarded as a minimum because many offenders are still active. For example 22 per cent of both males and females were convicted within the last five years. More accurate estimates will only be obtained when these cohorts are followed up further.

Estimating the rate of offending

The previous sections presented data on the duration of criminal careers, measured either by the number of convictions or the number of years an offender is active. From these two the rate at which offenders commit crimes per unit of time – usually taken to be one year – can be estimated. This measure is the rate λ in criminal careers terminology. Strictly λ is the rate at which offenders commit crimes while free to do so (defined as 'street time' in the U.S.) thus any time the offender spends in custody must be discounted. The rate at which an offender is committing crimes at various stages in his or her career is more informative than simply knowing whether an offender is active or not. λ is a key concept in criminal careers research and the focus of increasing research interest. There are several ways of estimating λ.

Upper bound to λ

A maximum value can be placed on the average value of λ for males by simply assuming that the male offenders who are apprehended in a year between them commit all the offences that are recorded by the police. As females commit fewer crimes than males it is also assumed that known male offenders commit all the crimes recorded apart from those known to have been committed by females. This procedure was followed to estimate λ for each of the years 1975, 1980, 1985 and 1990.

In 1975 the number of recorded crimes was 2,105,631. The number of females who were cautioned by the police or found guilty at court was 86,304. As it is assumed that they committed one crime each, that leaves 2,019,327 crimes. It is assumed therefore that all these crimes were committed by the 418,402 males who were given a police caution or found guilty at court. However, the average number of males in prison at any one time in 1975 was 38,601 and thus this number of offenders were prevented from committing crimes. The number of active male offenders was 379,801. Therefore for males, 2019327/379801 = 5.3.

1975 maximum average λ = 5.3 crimes per year

Similarly, using the same approach:-

1980 maximum average λ = 5.8 crimes per year

1985 maximum average λ = 7.5 crimes per year

1990 maximum average λ = 11.4 crimes per year

From the above it appears that λ has increased markedly between 1980 and 1990. However, this may not be so; it should be emphasised that these are the maximum average values. The higher 1990 figure reflects the decline in the number of persons found guilty or cautioned as a proportion of recorded crime (see Table 1.1).

Estimating rates for individual offenders

Although the method described above provides an upper estimate of the average value of λ it does not reveal how λ may vary between offenders. Another way of estimating λ is to look at the criminal histories of known offenders. However, λ cannot be measured directly unless self-report data are available. Information on arrests, court appearances or convictions can be obtained from criminal records and can be used to estimate μ, the annual rate of being arrested, appearing at court or being convicted. Assuming offenders who commit crimes have the same chance of being caught and convicted or cautioned, estimates of λ can be obtained from $\mu = \lambda q$ where q is the probability that a crime leads to conviction or caution. Estimates of q can be derived from criminal statistics (see Table 1.1) and were used to infer λ.

In order to calculate μ (or λ), the period in which an offender is active has to be identified. Blumstein and Cohen (1979) approached this issue by taking the period of time between the first and last arrest. They could assume therefore that an offender was active during the intervening period. By knowing the total number of arrests in this intervening period they could estimate μ_i. Their method can thus be expressed as:–

$$\mu_i = \frac{\text{Number of arrests between first and last arrest}}{\text{Time between first arrest and last arrest} - \text{total time spent in custody}} \qquad \text{Eq 4.1}$$

Brody and Tarling (1980) calculated annual rates of conviction for each of a sample of 770 sentenced prisoners, in prison in 1972 in the South East of England. (The sample and the results of this work are described in more detail in Chapter 9.)

The rate at which each prisoner was convicted while free μ_i was defined as:–

$$\mu_i = \frac{\text{Number of convictions}}{\text{Age at last conviction} - (\text{age of criminal responsibility} + \text{total length of time previously spent in custody})} \qquad \text{Eq 4.2}$$

Eq 4.2 was used to calculate μ_i for each prisoner. It was found that with the exception of one who had a conviction rate of 6.5 and another who had a rate of 14 per year, the maximum was 3 per year. The distribution was very highly skewed; 59 per cent of prisoners had been convicted less than once every two years.

A criticism can be levelled against Eq 4.2 in that it implicitly assumes that all offenders began their criminal careers at the age of criminal responsibility. Brody and Tarling assessed the adequacy of their formula and provided a prospective validation. Eq 4.2 was used to estimate the number of convictions that would be expected within one year and this estimate was compared with the actual number of reconvictions awarded to the sample. All but 41 prisoners in the sample were followed up for one year after release from prison and 254 (35 per cent of those followed up) were reconvicted within the period, some more than once. Between them they were convicted on 381 occasions. Using the formula, the number of convictions that would be expected (for those followed up) during one year is 418. This is a little higher than the actual number of subsequent convictions but 139 offenders were again sentenced to imprisonment and spent some of the follow up period in custody, thereby preventing them from committing further crimes leading to conviction. Thus Eq 4.2 has some empirical validity even if intuitively it is not correct. At least it avoids the problem of over–estimating μ_i by bounding the period of time by convictions. (Although Blumstein and Cohen do this they avoid over–estimating μ_i by eliminating the first and last arrest from the numerator of their equation.)

Further estimates of the rate of offending were derived for members of the 1953 cohort and for the sample of parolees. In both cases Eqs 4.1 and 4.2 were used to estimate the rate of convictions per year, μ_i, and offenders with just one conviction were excluded thus restricting the analyses to more active offenders. In addition, Eq 4.1 requires offenders to have at least 3 convictions – a first, a last and at least one in between. Estimates derived from this equation were thus confined to those with 3 or more convictions. Estimates of λ were then obtained from the relationship $\mu = \lambda q$. Summary results of the analyses are presented in Table 4.5.

Table 4.5
Annual rate of convictions, μ, annual rate of offending, λ

	1953 cohort males		*Parolees**		*1953 cohort females*	
	μ	λ	μ	λ	μ	λ
Average value						
Eq 4.1	0.9	2.8	1.2	3.7	0.9	2.8
Eq 4.2	0.5	1.6	0.8	2.5	0.3	0.9
Distribution**						
maximum value	11.0	34.2	5.6	17.4	5.5	17.1
90th percentile	1.9	5.9	1.6	5.0	2.1	6.5
Percentage $\mu < 0.5$ } $\lambda < 1.6$ }	37		29		63	

* For parolees only the number of court appearances was available. Values were increased by 1.4 to estimate convictions.

** The distribution is that produced by Eq 4.1.

It can be seen from Table 4.5 that Eq 4.1 produced higher estimates of the average value of μ and hence the average value of λ than Eq 4.2. This is partly due to the different samples; Eq 4.1 required offenders to have at least 3 convictions and the analysis was thereby restricted to more active offenders. In contrast estimates from Eq 4.2 included all offenders with at least 2 convictions. The difference is also due to the different denominator; the denominator in Eq 4.2 is the time between the last conviction and the age of criminal responsibility and is, in the vast majority of cases, much greater than the interval of time between the last conviction and the age of onset (age at first conviction). Nevertheless, despite being different in magnitude, the two estimates of μ were highly correlated. For example, for the sample of parolees the correlation coefficient between the estimates derived from each equation was 0.8.

Comparing the two samples of males, the parolees had higher average rates (μ = 1.2, λ = 3.7) than male offenders in the 1953 cohort (μ = 0.9, λ = 2.8) reflecting the fact that offenders in prison are in most cases more persistent offenders than offenders generally. It is interesting to note that μ and λ for females as estimated by Eq 4.1 were the same as for males in the 1953 cohort (μ = 0.9, λ = 2.8). The small group of females who were convicted on 3 or more occasions were convicted at the same rate as their male counterparts. This is in line with the results presented earlier; females who are convicted on a number of occasions are just as likely as males to be reconvicted.

Another feature in every sample is the variation in μ and λ between offenders and the skewness of the distributions. The 90th percentile value of μ and λ in each is not greatly above the average but a few offenders had much higher rates. The maximum values for males in the 1953 cohort were μ = 11.0, λ = 34.2, for male parolees, μ = 5.6, λ = 17.4 and for females μ = 5.5, λ = 17.1.

It should also be noted that the average values of λ obtained from the analyses of individual offenders are a good deal less than the upper bound values of λ presented earlier. The upper bound values are closer to the 90th percentiles.

Similar analyses have been undertaken in the United States and the results were presented in the report of the Panel on Criminal Careers (Blumstein *et. al*., 1986). Annual average arrests rates, μ for all index offences are not dissimilar to the annual rates of conviction presented here. Estimates from the various U.S. studies undertaken in different parts of the country ranged from about 0.6 to 1.2. In contrast estimates of λ in the U.S. are much higher; ranging from 9 to 13. However, when estimating the probability, q, the U.S. studies included unreported crimes measured by victim surveys. Only recorded crimes were included when estimating the value of q for this country.

Rates of offending at different ages

Does the rate of offending vary according to the age of the offender? The age–crime curve presented in Chapter 2 indicated that offending declines with age; for males, offending reaches a peak at 18 and falls away rapidly as age increases. There are two possible explanations for this relationship; first that most offenders begin their criminal careers in adolescence and cease to offend shortly after and/or, second, that offenders remain active but simply commit offences at a lower rate as they get older, that is μ declines with age. Evidence for the first explanation was given in Chapter 3 where it was shown that most offenders begin their careers in their youth and earlier in this chapter it was found that most careers are of a short duration.

Data for males and females in the 1953 cohort were analysed to assess the extent to which the rate of offending declines with age. The results are presented in Table 4.6.

Table 4.6
Rate of conviction by age, males and females, 1953 cohort

Age	*Number of offenders convicted*		*Number of convictions*		*Annual rate of convictions, μ*	
	males	*females*	*males*	*females*	*males*	*females*
9 < 14*	1901	172	2798	217	0.29	0.25
14 < 17	3421	384	5531	485	0.54	0.42
17 < 21	5950	661	10320	951	0.43	0.36
21 < 25	4091	551	7354	807	0.45	0.37
25 < 31	4030	761	6487	1111	0.27	0.24

* Although the age of criminal responsibility was 8 few 8 year olds were convicted. It therefore seems more realistic to start at age 9.

The analyses proceeded as follows. Any offender convicted between the ages of 9 and 14, was considered to be active throughout that 5 year period.

All the convictions that he or she received during that period were recorded. Thus 1,901 males were convicted and between them amassed 2,798 convictions between the ages 9 and 14. This means that on average they were convicted at a rate of 0.29 per year. The analysis was repeated for all other age groups.

It can be seen from the final column of Table 4.6 that the annual rate of offending for active offenders, both males and females, was lowest for the youngest (9 < 14) and oldest (25 < 31) age groups and higher for ages 14 to 25; the highest rates at age 14 < 17. Nevertheless, the results indicate, perhaps surprisingly, that active offenders, both males and females, commit offences at a fairly constant rate for much of their careers.

Confirmation of this result is found in other studies. Farrington (1983) carried out a similar analysis on offenders in his London cohort and found little variation in rates of offending at different ages. However, he only considered age up to the mid-twenties and so would not have observed any decline after that age. This London cohort was the subject of a different kind of analysis by Barnett et. al., (1987). They examined the time intervals between convictions and found them to be consistent with the hypothesis that the annual rate of offending is constant over time. (This analysis was the precursor to fitting different stochastic models and is discussed further in Chapter 7.) Blumstein and Cohen (1979) (see also Blumstein *et. al.*, 1988) found, for a group of offenders in Washington D.C., that arrest rates were relatively stable with age for active offenders.

Thus from the analyses so far undertaken it would seem that the shape of the age–crime curve is due more to participation, that is how many offenders are active at different ages, rather than the rate at which active offenders commit offences at different ages.

Age of onset and rate of offending

Earlier in this chapter it was shown that the number of convictions varied inversely with the age of onset; the earlier an offender began his/her criminal career the more convictions he/she was likely to amass. But do offenders who begin their careers early commit crimes at a higher rate per year or is their greater number of convictions simply attributable to the longer time at which they are criminally active? To answer this question the average rate of convictions, μ, was plotted against the age at first conviction for males and females in the 1953 cohort. μ, as estimated by Eq 4.2, did show a steady decline with age of onset but this is to be expected given the demonimator of Eq 4.2 which does not take into account the age at which an offender began his career. μ derived from Eq 4.1, reveals a different pattern which is shown in Figure 4.3.

It can be seen that, in contrast to Figure 4.1 (which depicted a steady decline in the number of convictions the later the career began) Figure 4.3 indicates that the rate of being convicted per year is less dependent on the age at first conviction. For males μ is fairly constant or increases slightly. (The last few years are distorted somewhat; the analysis being restricted to the few offenders who were convicted several times in a short space of time.) The graph for females depicts a similar trend but being based on small numbers fluctuates more from year to year.

The relationship between age of onset and the rate at which offenders commit crime is considered again in Chapter 7.

Figure 4.3
Average annual rate of conviction by age at first conviction

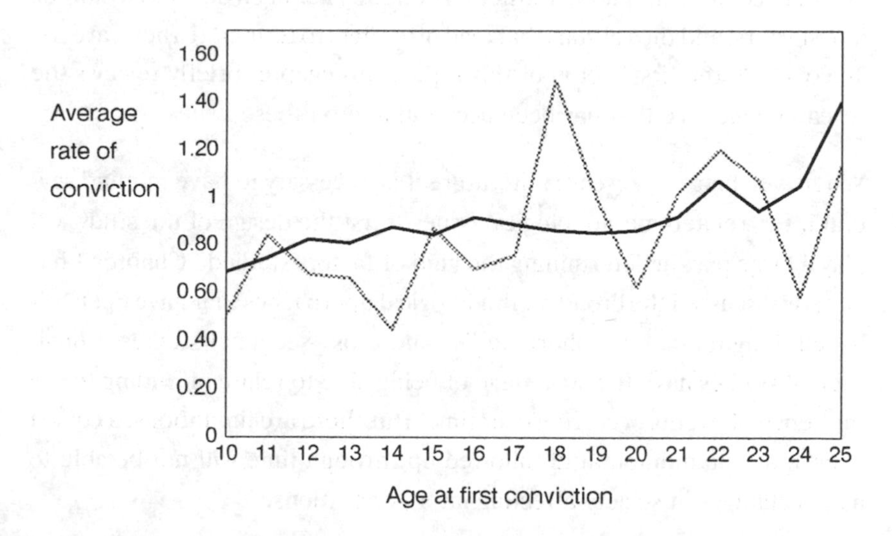

5 FACTORS ASSOCIATED WITH OFFENDING

The evidence presented so far has revealed a variety of criminal careers. Some people do not become delinquent while others do. But even amongst offenders, there is considerable variation in the intensity of offending and career development. Many people commit crime once or very occasionally then stop. Others go on to become persistent offenders into adult life. Furthermore, many offenders begin their careers while juveniles but a significant proportion are 'late starters'. The criminal career approach highlights these variations in patterns of offending and suggests that different explanations may be required for different sorts of offenders. For example, the reasons why people become delinquent in the first place may be different to the reasons why some persist or develop extensive criminal careers. The research evidence is patchy; most studies have concentrated on juvenile offending, discriminating between those who do and those who do not become delinquent. Rather less enquiry has been devoted to adults, late starters, and the reasons that lead offenders to terminate their careers. To conclude the first secton of this report this chapter briefly reviews the research evidence that has been accumulated on these issues.

When weighing the research literature it is necessary to have in mind several inter-related methodological issues. First the design of the study will play a large part in determining the kind of factors studied. Chapter 1 has already discussed the broad methodological approaches that have been followed; longitudinal or cohort studies and cross-sectional studies. Longitudinal studies have the advantage of being able to relate offending to the influence of events occurring over time. But there are limitations; a cohort chosen at one moment and followed up through time will not be able to assess changes in society affecting later generations.

The second point, regardless of the methodological approach, relates to the analyses undertaken. Many factors are themselves interrelated and sorting out their relative importance requires a multivariate approach to analysing the data. Emphasis here will thus be placed on any multivariate analysis undertaken. The need to assess factors in the context of controlling for the influences of others is apparent, for example, in the assessment of the relationship between unemployment and crime. Tarling (1982) reviewed about 30 studies and found that the strength of the relationship between unemployment and crime was much reduced when other factors, such as age, and social class, were included in the analysis. "The complex inter-relationship between unemployment and other socio-democratic indicators makes it extremely difficult to disentangle the independent effects of unemployment".

It is outside the scope of this report to summarise all the research that has been conducted on offending. Comprehensive reviews can be found in Loeber and Dishion (1983), Rutter and Giller (1983), Visher and Roth (1986) and Wilson and Herrnstein (1985). The aim here is more modest; to highlight the main factors associated with offending, to give priority to research conducted in this country and to summarise the research undertaken since the above, comprehensive, reviews were completed. New information is presented on co-offending, that is, the extent to which offenders act alone or with others.

Factors associated with participation in offending

Participation rates were the subject of Chapter 3 where it was shown that males are more likely to participate in crime than females. Little more will be said here about the basic sex differentials although the factors associated with both male and female delinquency are discussed. Age too is related to involvement in crime and this has been discussed elsewhere in this report, particularly in Chapter 2. The findings will not be repeated here.

Most of the research on the factors related to participation in crime has considered juveniles and young adults but it was pointed out in Chapter 3 that one quarter of males in the 1953 Research and Statistics Department cohort who received a conviction before age 31 were 21 or over before they began their careers. What limited information is available on late starters will be presented at the end of this section.

Early problem behaviour

Evidence of early 'troublesome' or 'anti-social' behaviour has consistently been found to be a precursor of subsequent delinquency. Evidence has been gathered from parents, teachers and social workers.

Mitchell and Rosa (1981) examined data for 642 boys aged between 5 and 15 years attending schools in Buckinghamshire. They compared parents' and teachers' assessments of the boys' behaviour with subsequent court appearance (by age 20) for an indictable offence. Various aspects of problem behaviour were found to be related to criminality: stealing, destructiveness, wandering from home and lying were positively related to criminality whereas excessive worrying and food fads were negatively related. Thus two out of three boys described by their parents as having "stolen things on several occasions" subsequently appeared in court compared with one in five of those not so described. However, not only were those so described more likely to have been convicted of theft offences, as might be expected, but they were also five times more likely to be convicted of damage to property and seven times more likely to be convicted of violence offences. Those considered destructive were also more likely to be convicted of theft, damage and violence, but those likely to wander from home, though more likely to be convicted of theft offences, were not more likely to be convicted of damage or violence. Parents and teachers did not always classify the boys in the same way but those boys who were classified identically by parents and teachers were more likely to become delinquent.

In Ouston's (1984) study teachers were asked to rate their pupils' behaviour. The study comprised 1,317 boys and 1,035 girls attending 12 inner-London secondary schools. A higher percentage of those boys and girls rated by teachers as 'anti-social' compared with other children received a police caution or a conviction at court. Thus for girls, 22.9 per cent of the anti-social group became delinquent compared with 4.1 per cent of other girls and 60.3 per cent of anti-social boys became delinquent compared with 22.6 per cent of other boys. This relationship persisted in a multivariate analysis which controlled for other background factors; intelligence, occupation of parent and ethnic origin.

In the Cambridge Study of Delinquent Development (a cohort study of about 400 males from a working class area of London) a measure of 'troublesomeness' at ages 8–10 derived from teachers and classmates was found to be a good predictor of subsequent criminal behaviour. Of the 92 males categorised as 'most troublesome', 44.6 per cent became juvenile delinquents. This compares with only 3.5 per cent of the 143 males classified as 'least troublesome' and 21.6 per cent of the 176 'moderately troublesome' (West, 1982). In a later follow-up of this cohort, Farrington (1983) found other aspects which discriminated criminals from non-criminals at age 25, such as daring, aggressiveness and hostile attitudes when juveniles.

Truancy can be seen as another form of problem behaviour and it has been found to be closely related to troublesomeness and other measures of disruptive behaviour. Not surprisingly, therefore, truancy has been found to be related to delinquency. West and Farrington (1973), Belson (1975), and May (1975) all found for boys, and Wadsworth (1979) and Ouston (1984) for boys and girls, that truants were more likely to become delinquents than non-truants or, that delinquents were more likely to have records of persistent absenteeism or truancy.

Despite the persistent association of early problem behaviour with criminal behaviour found in these studies (and further indirect evidence is available from other research) there are difficulties of interpretation. Firstly there is a methodological point. Ouston, herself, admits that there may be some problems with using teachers' ratings as an independent predictor. If teachers are aware of the child's criminal record that knowledge may in turn affect their assessment of behaviour. In fact, by the time teachers completed their assessment, one-third of the delinquent girls and a half of the delinquent boys had already been cautioned or convicted. This may also be a problem in the Mitchell and Rosa study although it should be noted that teachers' assessments in the Cambridge study ante-date criminal behaviour. Secondly, there is a more substantive issue when assessing the causal relationship between problem behaviour and crime. As West (1982) states, for purely predictive purposes assessments of troublesomeness "works well" and better than most other variables, "but that, of course, tells one nothing about how such behaviour originates". Crime can be thought of as one form of anti-social or troublesome behaviour. These different behavioural traits may simply be different manifestations eminating from the same causal factors.

Family circumstances

Researchers have considered the impact on criminal behaviour of various aspects of family circumstances, structure and family functioning. The most important of these are considered in turn.

i) Parenting skills and family management techniques

Weak relationships between parents and children (little communication and affection) and a lack of child rearing skills, such as absence of appropriate discipline or rules, little interest in children's activities or schooling, and ineffective supervision have been shown to be related to 'troublesomeness' and subsequent delinquency. Several studies have attempted to measure 'parental performance' directly and these studies are discussed first.

Wadsworth's (1979) study, comprising just over 5,000 persons born in 1946, found that teachers' assessments of parental interest in a son's progress at school was inversely related to participation in crime. The more interest parents took in their son's schooling (as measured by the teachers) the less likely it was that the son would be convicted. At primary school, 25 per cent of boys whose parents were rated lowest became delinquent compared with 7.5 per cent of those rated highest. Even greater differences were found at the secondary school stage, 34.2 per cent and 8 per cent respectively. This relationship persisted in a multivariate analysis controlling for social class and other aspects of family size and structure.

In their study of families in Newcastle, Miller *et. al.* (1974) analysed the records of 63 children (mostly boys) who were convicted before their fifteenth birthday and found what they called a 'marked deficiency of good parentcraft'. By this they meant a father or mother who was not rated highly as kind and effective or one who showed less than average interest in his or her children's development. Lewis *et. al.* (1982) also found a relationship between an index of fathers' 'participation' with their children in early life and subsequent delinquency. Children who had had a good relationship with their fathers were less likely to acquire a criminal record.

West (1982) found that about one-third of boys in the London cohort whose parents had been assessed by social workers to have performed their child-rearing duties unsatisfactorily became juvenile delinquents. This was about twice the rate for boys from other families.

Riley and Shaw (1985) examined the influence of parental supervision. They asked parents of their national sample of about 750 14 and 15 year old boys and girls how often they knew who their son or daughter was with, where they were going and what they were doing. This measure of parental supervision was related to self-report offending: higher supervision resulted in lower delinquency. However, for the boys this relationship disappeared in a multivariate analysis controlling for delinquent friends, attitudes towards crime and attitudes towards their father. On the other hand, parental supervision remained an important factor for girls after controlling for other variables. But, as Riley and Shaw found, parents had different ideas about the appropriate levels of supervision for their sons and daughters. Daughters received much higher levels of supervision.

ii) Family disruption

In addition to direct assessments of parental performance, as above, there are other factors to be considered which may affect the quality of parenting and hence the chances of children becoming offenders. Examples are disruption of the family and discord within it. Wadsworth (1979) examined various indicators of disruption of family life. Break-up of the family, separation or divorce (but *not* death of a parent) nearly doubled the chances that the son would be convicted of an offence by age 21. The age that the break occurred was also found to be important: family breaks early in a child's life were more likely to result in subsequent criminal behaviour. Family disruption was also a factor in discriminating delinquent girls from non-delinquent girls in Wadsworth's study.

Farrington (1983) also found that family disruption, as measured by separation from a parent or a broken home, nearly doubled the chances of cohort members becoming offenders by age 25.

In contrast to the effects on criminality caused by permanent disruptions (separation or divorce) no researcher has demonstrated any strong relationship between criminality and temporary disruptions caused by the mother being in full time employment (Wadsworth, 1979, West and Farrington, 1973 and Miller *et. al.*, 1974).

iii) Family size and structure

West (1982) found that family size was one of five key factors associated with delinquency in the Cambridge Study of Delinquent Development. Of boys from large families (four or more children) 32.3 per cent became juvenile delinquents, which was about twice the rate for children from smaller families.

Wadsworth (1979) also found family size related to delinquency. The proportion of boys with no siblings convicted (9.1 per cent) was little different from boys with one or two siblings (10 per cent). In contrast 24.3 per cent of children with three or more siblings were convicted. However, this association was statistically significant only in the 'manual' social group.

Wadsworth went on to consider other aspects of family structure. He found that the child's position in the family was related to delinquency: first born children were less likely to become delinquent, fourth and later born most likely. The chances of participating in crime increased with further family growth after the subject's birth. (Miller *et. al.*, 1974, also found that the families of delinquent children tended to be larger, suggesting that size reduces family effectiveness.) The likelihood of being convicted declined steadily as the length of time spent as an only child increased. There was also a greater likelihood of delinquency amongst boys and girls whose mothers had married early (before 20) or late (over 30). But the likelihood of criminality diminished the longer parents were married before having children.

Family size is thus important, though its impact is complex and not altogether clear. Family size is not found to be related to delinquency in middle-class families. This suggests that it is other inter-related factors in poorer families, such as family income and poor housing which can lead to weaker parental supervision and control and exacerbate the "disadvantages which tend to accompany family size in poorer sections of the community" (Rutter and Giller, 1983).

Furthermore, as Wadsworth recognised, larger families are likely to have worse environmental and housing conditions and it is this that leads to greater delinquency. Nevertheless, a multivariate analysis controlling for environmental factors still showed that family size and birth order were related to delinquency. In the light of this result he concluded that maternal attention and parent-child relationships exerted an independent effect on the likelihoood of delinquency.

Parent and sibling criminality

Delinquent children are more likely to have delinquent parents and/or delinquent siblings. This result has been found consistently in a range of studies although most of them were undertaken outside this country. The main support here comes from the Cambridge Study of Delinquent Development (Osborn and West, 1979, West, 1982 and Farrington, 1983). The risk of a member of the cohort aquiring a conviction by his twenty-third birthday more than doubled if his father had a conviction. If other family members were convicted this also increased the chances of criminality in sons. Furthermore, the son's chances of being convicted were three and a half times greater if he had more than two other family members with a criminal record than if he belonged to a conviction free family.

The family transmission of criminality, is difficult to interpret. Genetic factors or labelling (the result of the family being known to the police) may both play a part. But other factors may also be relevant such as family disadvantage and parental inadequacies, exhibited by these families. It may be that criminal parents set aggressive or anti-social (if not actually criminal) models of behaviour for their offspring to follow.

Delinquent peers and co-offending

Associating with delinquent peers has been found to be related to criminal behaviour. For example, in the Cambridge Study of Delinquent Development 59 per cent of males who had delinquent friends at age 14 had a conviction themselves by age 25, whereas only 25 per cent of those without delinquent associates were convicted. Gladstone (1978) also found that acts of vandalism were more likely to be committed by groups. He makes the point, however, that most boys are members of gangs or associate with others but that it is members of what he defined as 'tough groups' (in which it was important to be tough) that were most likely to commit vandalism. Riley and Shaw (1985) found that boys who reported their friends were relatively more involved in delinquency were about eight times as likely to be delinquent themselves.

Peer group influences were also examined by Shapland (1978). If any of the 51 boys (aged 13–14) admitted to any offence he was asked whether he committed it alone, or with other boys, girls or adults. No boy admitted committing offences with girls and few with adults. The majority of offences were committed by groups of boys (60 per cent), and 30 per cent by boys on their own.

Reiss (1986) and Reiss and Farrington (1991) reviewed the research on co-offending. It seems to suggest that group offending is more common at younger ages and the size of the group or the extent of co-offending declines with age. Acting alone becomes the dominant form of offending by the mid-twenties. The extent of group offending also varies with the type of offence committed and by the criminal history of the offender. (Knight and West, 1975, for example, found that offenders with more extensive criminal careers were more likely to commit offences alone than less serious offenders.)

Data for the sample of offenders convicted at the Crown Court enabled some of these hypotheses to be examined further. For each defendant in the sample details of all co-defendants were recorded and Tables 5.1 and 5.2 show the extent to which co-defendants were involved. The data are presented for different types of offence, and by the age and sex of the defendant.

Table 5.1
Principal offence, by sex and number of co-defendants

	Male defendants		*Female defendants*	
Type of offence	*per cent convicted alone*	*Average number of co-defendants*	*per cent convicted alone*	*Average number of co-defendants*
Violence against the person	72	0.5	83	0.4
Sexual offences	97	0.0	100	0.0
Robbery	48	0.8	40	1.3
Burglary	62	0.7	69	1.3
Theft and handling stolen goods	70	0.5	69	0.5
Fraud and forgery	74	0.4	52	1.4
Criminal damage	68	0.6	82	0.2
Drug offences	62	1.1	71	0.4
Motoring offences	98	0.0	100	0.0
Other	72	0.6	70	1.5
Total	69	0.5	69	0.7

It can be seen from Table 5.1 that exactly the same proportion of male and female defendants were convicted alone (69 per cent) and that the proportion varied somewhat by type of offence. Sexual offences and motoring offences were invariably committed alone. In contrast, for males, robbery, burglary and drug offences tended to involve groups of offenders. When groups were involved they tended to be larger in the case of drug offences than in the case of offences of robbery – hence the higher average number of co-defendants in drug offences. For female defendants robbery and offences of fraud and forgery were more likely to be committed by a single offender although on the occasions when co-offenders were involved there tended to be more of them. (It should be noted that there were fewer female defendants in the sample and the conclusions that can be drawn are less certain.)

Table 5.2
Age of defendant, by sex and number of co-defendants

Age of defendants	*Male defendants* per cent convicted alone	*Male defendants* Average number of co-defendants	*Female defendants* per cent convicted alone	*Female defendants* Average number of co-defendants
10 < 17	35	1.1	33	1.7
17 < 21	64	0.7	67	0.7
21 < 25	67	0.6	68	0.8
25 < 30	72	0.5	74	0.6
30 < 35	73	0.4	58	0.7
35 < 40	80	0.3	71	0.4
40 < 45	82	0.3	85	0.3
45+	79	0.3	80	0.7
Total	69	0.5	69	0.7

Further analysis considered the interaction between type of offence, age of defendants and the number of co-defendants. In Chapter 2 it was pointed out that age is related to the type of offence committed. It could be, therefore, that the decline in co-offending with age is a result of the different kinds of offences committed by offenders of different ages. However, this did not seem to be the case. Generally, the decline in co-offending with age persisted within each type of offence.

An interesting exception is criminal damage. For this type of offence only 20 per cent of juvenile defendants (those under 17 years of age) acted alone and only 44 per cent of young adults (age 17 less than 21). However, for 21 to 25 year olds the proportion acting alone had risen to 85 per cent and for 25 year olds and over to 90 per cent. These findings reflect the wide variety of criminal damage offences which range from less serious vandalism committed by groups of young offenders to offences stemming from different causes committed by older adults acting alone. Looking through some of the case papers it became clear that criminal damage offences committed by older offenders were more akin to crimes of violence and often arose following provocation, arguments or disputes. In one case a father was denied access to his children by his wife's co-habitee and his response was to damage property within the house and the cars parked outside. Another incident stemmed from provocation and an argument with a shopkeeper.

It was also possible with these data to analyse the relationship between criminal history and the number of co-defendants. For both males and females the proportion of first offenders convicted alone was near the average for all offenders (67 per cent for males and 70 per cent for females). However, for male offenders with previous convictions there was a tendency for the proportion of defendants who acted alone to increase with the number of previous convictions. A similar relationship, but not so clear cut, emerged for females. The results are presented in Table 5.3.

Table 5.3
Number of previous convictions, by sex and proportion of defendants convicted alone

Number of previous convictions	*Male defendants* *per cent convicted alone*	*Female defendants* *per cent convicted alone*
0 (first offenders)	67	70
1	61	62
2	61	67
3	64	65
4	65	78
5	70	78
6 or more	77	74

It can be seen that offenders were much more likely to commit offences on their own if they had an extensive criminal record.

Finally, it was possible to consider the sex of co-defendants and the extent to which males and females were jointly involved in crimes. It has already been pointed out that the same proportion of males and females acted alone (69 per cent). The remaining 31 per cent acted with one or more other persons. For males who had co-defendants, only about 10 per cent were females whereas males made up 57 per cent of the co-defendants of those females who did not act alone. Thus, to that extent men are more involved in female crime than vice versa. It was shown in Chapter 2 that females were much less likely than males to commit certain offences, notably sexual offences, robbery and burglary, suggesting that these are male offences. It might be thought, therefore, that when females are involved in such offences it is because of their association or attachment to groups of males engaged in such crimes. McClintock and Avison (1968) suggest that females are usually involved in their criminal activities with male offenders but this claim has not been fully investigated. There is some weak evidence for this in the sample but not as much as might have been expected. On several occasions one female committed a robbery or a burglary with a group of men but it was not the case that females only committed these offences with males.

Social class and family income

It is usually assumed that offending is much more widespread amongst persons of lower social status. Miller *et. al.* (1974) found 'a clear excess of delinquent children from families from social classes IV and V'. Wadsworth (1979) in his national sample found that 4 per cent of sons of 'upper-middle' families had become delinquent by age 21 compared with 21.9 per cent of sons from 'lower-manual' families. Class differences were only apparent at these extremes; both the 'lower-middle' and the 'upper-manual' groups had participation rates of 12 per cent.

Ouston (1984) also found a relationship between social class and delinquency for both boys and girls although it was more pronounced for boys. For example, the proportion of boys who received a police caution or were convicted by age 18 was 17.3 per cent if the main breadwinner was in the professional, managerial and skilled non-manual group, 26.8 per cent if in the skilled manual group and 35.4 per if in the semi-skilled and unskilled manual group. The corresponding figures for girls were 1.6 per cent, 4.1 per cent and 7.5 per cent respectively.

These studies, based on official records of offending (police cautions or convictions at court), generally indicate class differentials in offending, but self-report studies find the association between social status and offending to be much weaker. Gladstone (1978) found that among boys whose fathers had unskilled or semi-skilled jobs 42 per cent reported a high involvement in vandalism as against 30 per cent of those whose fathers had higher status jobs. In contrast, Mawby (1980) and Riley and Shaw (1985) found no evidence that offending varied with social class (but too much reliance should not be placed on Mawby's study so far as social class is concerned – the sample was mainly drawn from a working class neighbourhood).

The narrower differences generally found in self-report studies compared with studies based on official records has led some to conclude that the class differences observed in the latter are more a reflection of official agencies' response to offending than a measure of its actual occurrence. But, as noted earlier in this report, self-report studies have in the main included only minor offences. Self-report studies are, therefore, important in confirming that minor infractions are prevalent amongst people from all social classes but they do not necessarily refute the findings of 'official' studies. In fact, studies of official offending also show that the differences between the social classes are much narrower for minor crimes.

As most of the boys in West's (1982) study came from lower social classes (the cohort was drawn from a working class area of London) social class did not discriminate offenders from non-offenders too well (although a relationship was evident). However, family income, which was related to social class, had a much stronger effect and was found to be a key factor: 33.3 per cent of boys from low income families became juvenile delinquents compared with 16.7 per cent of boys from higher income families.

Intelligence and educational achievement

Low intelligence, however measured, and poor school performance or achievement have been identified as important factors in discriminating delinquents from non-delinquents.

Wadsworth (1979) found that boys classified by primary school teachers as 'poor or lazy workers' when they were 10 years old were more likely to become delinquent than boys regarded as 'very hard' or 'hard workers'. A similar classification made by secondary school teachers when the boys were 13 and 15 was also found to be related to delinquency. In addition, the boys and girls were given various intelligence tests at age 8, 11, and 15. Below average performance in them was associated with delinquency but this relationship disappeared when background variables such as social class or birth order had been taken into acount.

West (1982) found that below average intelligence was related to delinquency: 31.1 per cent of such boys were convicted as juveniles, about twice the proportion of other boys. Furthermore, this relationship was also found when delinquency was measured by self-report. Self-report delinquents tended to score low on intelligence tests and educational attainment In contrast to Wadsworth's findings, intelligence remained an important factor in a multivariate analysis controlling for other factors.

The boys and girls in Ouston's (1984) sample were given various reading and non-verbal tests. For both boys and girls the delinquents had lower scores than non-delinquents. Further confirmation comes from Miller *et. al.* (1974). Their delinquents performed less well than other children on a range of intelligence tests.

Ouston also looked at educational attainment. She found that the delinquents did less well in examinations; over a half of delinquents obtained no grades compared with a quarter of non-delinquents. This result is not surprising given the delinquents' poorer performance on the intelligence tests, their worse behaviour at school and poorer attendance.

Alcohol consumption

Some crimes are defined in terms of alcohol consumption such as drunkenness and drink-driving offences. To this extent, at least, alcohol is a factor in crime causation. Research interest relates to whether alcohol has a causal effect in other types of crime - particularly public disorder incidents and crimes of violence. But causation is not all one way. There is at least a little evidence to suggest that some offenders deliberately avoid drinking when intending to commit certain property offences. Burglars interviewed by Bennett and Wright (1984) said that they purposely did not drink before an offence as it impaired their performance.

From surveys of alcohol consumption it is known that many people drink, with the heaviest drinkers being young men age 16 to 24. It is also this group that is mainly responsible for committing crime. Furthermore, research shows that almost one half the incidents of disorderly behaviour dealt with by the police occur shortly after permitted drinking hours. They are more likely to occur on Friday and Saturday nights and to involve young men (Ramsay 1982, Hope 1985, Tuck 1989).

Gottfredson (1984), using self-report data collected from the 1982 British Crime Survey on the amount of alcohol consumed, found that 'heavy' drinkers were more likely to report that they had committed one or more offences. The heavy drinkers were eight times more likely than others to report having committed offences of violence (16 per cent and 2 per cent respectively).

West and Farrington (1977) also found that those members of their cohort who had been convicted by age 18 or 19 were more likely than the non-delinquents to say that they were heavy drinkers, to become aggressive after drinking and to become involved in fights.

Mott (1987) discusses the nature of any causal relationship between alcohol and crime. Whilst not dismissing the 'direct causal' effects of alcohol on behaviour she suggests that it is "most likely that the consumption of alcohol is only one of a number of factors which interact to increase the probability that, on a particular drinking occasion, a drinker will commit a crime. These factors include the cultural and sub-cultural attitudes to particular settings and situations in which alcohol is consumed, the behaviour expected in the circumstances, as well as the social and individual characteristics of the drinker".

There is evidence that a young lifestyle which includes a great deal of drinking in pubs and clubs provides an important link between alcohol and violent crime and of disorderly behaviour falling short of serious violence (see Mott 1990). West and Farrington (1977) found offenders "less socially restrained, more hedonistic, more impulsive, more reckless as well as more aggressive than their non-delinquent peers. They smoked more, they drank more and gambled more. They had a faster life-style, they went out more, they visited bars, discotheques and parties more often".

Key factors identified in the Cambridge Study of Delinquent Development

Many of the influences reviewed above are inter-related and some have been included in some studies but not others. In an attempt to sort out the more important factors West (1982) conducted a detailed multivariate analysis. From this he identified five key factors that were associated with a member of his cohort becoming delinquent.

1. Coming from a low-income family. 33.3 per cent became juvenile delinquents compared with 16.7 per cent of the rest of the sample.
2. Coming from a large family. 32.3 per cent became juvenile delinquents.
3. Having parents considered by social workers to have performed the child-rearing duties unsatisfactorily. 32.3 per cent became juvenile delinquents.
4. Having below average intelligence. 31.1 per cent became juvenile delinquents compared with 15.9 per cent in the rest of the sample.
5. Having a parent with a criminal record. 37.9 per cent became juvenile delinquents compared with 14.6 per cent in the rest of the sample.

Because of the extensive overlap of adverse circumstances a substantial minority of 63 boys (15% of the cohort) had a combination of at least three of the above five factors. Almost one half of this group became juvenile delinquents compared with only a fifth of the sample as a whole (West, 1982).

Race

In contrast to the United States there has been little systematic research in this country examining the participation of different ethnic groups in crime. The standard distinction drawn in American research is between white and black people, but race is more diverse than that dichotomy implies. In recent years more attention has been paid to hispanics in America and Asians in this country as significant groups.

Many of the birth cohort studies discussed so far originated at a time when there were few ethnic minorities in Britain. Thus, for example, the cohort comprising the Cambridge Study on Delinquent Development, (West, 1982), and the cohort assembled by Wadsworth (1979) contain no members from ethnic minorities and can provide no information on the relationship between race and crime.

A few studies (Bottoms, 1967, 1973; Lambert, 1970), were conducted at a time when first generation immigrants were arriving in Britain. They found that non-white groups were less likely to offend than whites. More recent evidence, however, has indicated that the pattern has been changing.

For several years the Metropolitan Police classified people arrested according to their skin colour and the data for 1987 were presented in Home Office (1989a). Earlier data are also discussed by Walker (1987). In 1987 'white skinned' persons comprised 85 per cent of the population living in the Metropolitan Police District but only 72 per cent of those arrested. Asians comprised 4 per cent of those arrested, slightly less than their proportion in the population (5 per cent). In sharp contrast 'black skinned' persons were over-represented in the arrest statistics. While such persons comprised 5 per cent of the population they accounted for 18 per cent of the arrests. The disproportion was more marked for some types of offences; 54 per cent of those arrested for robbery and other violent theft, 21 per cent of those arrested for assaults and, similarly, 17 per cent arrested for burglary were classified as 'black skinned'.

There are some problems with these data when assessing participation in crime. Firstly, it may be that some of the difference between the groups reflects the different probabilities of being arrested. For instance, it is known that blacks are more likely than whites to be stopped and stops often lead to arrest. Of course, this fact does not resolve whether blacks are stopped because they commit more crime or because the police exercise their discretionary powers differently. The second, more important criticism of the arrest data is that they do not include any information on other factors such as social class or educational achievements. It is thus not possible to undertake any multivariate analysis to assess the impact of race while controlling for background factors. The only study to have considered race and crime in this way is Ouston (1984) and her study is important for this reason.

Ouston's (1984) sample comprised 1,317 boys and 1,035 girls born between 1 September 1959 and 31 August 1960 attending 12 Inner London schools. Information was collected on all indictable and non-indictable offences committed by the pupils up to March 1978 (when they were in their seventeenth year) which resulted in a police caution or conviction at court. Ouston found that 28.0 per cent of the 982 boys whose parents were born in the UK or Eire were cautioned or convicted. A lower proportion was found for boys whose parents were born in Cyprus (21 per cent of 109) or India or Pakistan (24 per cent of 17) but higher for boys born of West Indian parents (39 per cent of 161). A similar pattern emerged for the girls; 5.1 per cent of the 752 girls born of UK or Eire parents became delinquent, 1.1 per cent of the 93 girls whose parents were born in Cyprus became delinquent, none of the 17 girls whose parents were born in India or Pakistan but a much higher proportion, 12.5 per cent, of the 152 girls whose parents were born in the West Indies became delinquent.

Ouston went on to conduct a series of multivariate analyses. Because of the small number of delinquent girls the analyses were confined to boys. Similarly boys of Asian or Cypriot parents were excluded because of small samples or because of the absence of sufficient background information. The analyses therefore focussed on two groups of boys; those with parents born in the UK or Eire, and those with parents born in the West Indies. The other variables included in the analyses were social class, intelligence and teachers' assessment of behaviour. Teachers' assessment and social class produced an adequate 'fit' (or explanation) of the data. Given the possible problems with teachers' assessment (discussed earlier) Ouston excluded this variable and repeated the analysis. In this second analysis intelligence and social class proved to be adequate. Thus, in the multivariate analyses, ethnic origin was not a significant factor contributing to the explanation of delinquency once social class, teachers' ratings and intelligence were controlled for.

Ouston's sample contained few Asian boys and girls, whereas Mawby's *et. al*. (1979), being based in Bradford, provided more reliable information on Asian crime rates. Mawby *et. al*. analysed data on known juvenile offenders (boys and girls) in Bradford for the years 1974 to 1977. Information on police cautions and convictions at court were gathered. Relating these data to the resident population, they found that for 1976 the rate of offenders per 100 juveniles in the city was 3.2 for Asians compared with 6.3 for non-Asians; giving a non-Asian to Asian ratio of 2:1. (It should be pointed out that this is not strictly a participation rate as a juvenile could have more than one caution or conviction.) Unfortunately no information was available on the types of crime committed by the juveniles and no background information was available to permit any multivariate analysis. Nevertheless the lower rates for Asians accord with Ouston's results. Mawby *et. al*. also make the point that Asians in Bradford are to be found predominantly in the most disadvantaged areas so that their lower crime rates are even more remarkable. They suggest that cultural factors and the influence of the family protect Asians from crime.

The evidence on participation in crime by different ethnic minorities is limited to two studies and only two areas of the country, London and Bradford. Furthermore, both studies were restricted to official statistics, police cautions and convictions at court. No self-report studies have been undertaken. These two studies indicate that Asians may be less likely to commit crime whereas West Indians may be more likely to do so although, for the latter group, this is no more than would be expected given their generally adverse social conditions.

Late starters

Juveniles and young adults have been the focus of much of the research cited above. This research has examined the reasons why some commit crime and some do not. Relatively little attention has been given to why people, having escaped the crime prone years of adolescence, commit criminal offences in later life. Yet this is an important and significant group. It was noted in Chapter 3 that nearly a quarter of the male offenders in the 1953 cohort did not start their career until after their 21st birthday.

The only information on late starters in this country is available from West (1982). He examined the background of the 33 males in his cohort who were first convicted between the ages of 18 and 25 and compared them with the group who had been convicted before 18 and the group of non-delinquents, that is those who were not convicted before age 25. Examining the three groups on the five key factors identified and listed above, West found that the late starters were closer to the non-delinquents than the juvenile delinquents. For example, only 12.1 per cent of the latecomers had more than two of the five key factors compared with 38 per cent of the group convicted before age 18 and 7.5 per cent of the non-delinquents. Thus late starters had not suffered adverse factors to the same extent as juvenile delinquents. The only exception was that as a group the late starters had low intelligence scores at ages 8 to 10; their scores being similar to those of the juvenile delinquents. Furthermore, a high proportion of the late starters had been rated 'troublesome' at school and the self-reported offending for this group (measured at ages 14 and 16) was also higher than for non-delinquents.

From interviews with them, West formed the impression that late starters tended to be less committed to crime than juvenile offenders. They were reluctant to identify themselves as criminals; they often denied their guilt and felt that they had been treated harshly by the police and the courts.

High rate offenders

Most research has focussed on discriminating offenders from non-offenders. But Chapter 4 highlighted the fact that a small proportion of offenders commit a disproportionate number of crimes. What factors, if any, discriminate high rate offenders who go on to commit many crimes from those who just commit one or two and then end their careers? Research on recidivists and 'chronic' or persistent offenders provides some information. Before presenting results it is necessary to clarify the approaches that this research has taken, or might take. The particular issue here is the point in a career at which the high rate offenders are identified.

The first approach has attempted to identify prospectively and at an early age which children will go on to become persistent offenders, perhaps into adult life.

West (1982) compared the 36 men in his London cohort who were defined as 'persisting recidivists' with the rest of the sample – 'non-persisting recidivists' and 'non-offenders'. (The persisting recidivists were defined as those men who had received two or more convictions before age 19 and had received at least one further conviction during the following five years.) The factors included in the analysis were those measured at age 10 or earlier. In common with other studies (Wadsworth, 1979, Mitchell and Rosa, 1981 and Ouston, 1984), West found that the factors that distinguished persisting recidivists from other men in the cohort were the same as those that distinguished *all* offenders from non-offenders (discussed earlier in this chapter). There was a difference, however, in that the persisting recidivists were found to have even more extreme ratings on measures of adversity. The persisting recidivists were thus even more likely to have received poor parenting, to have the lowest IQ, to come from very large families with the lowest family incomes, to have both parents convicted and to have been exceptionally troublesome at school.

Blumstein *et. al*. (1985) also analysed data from the London cohort. (Some information from this study was presented in Chapter 4.) The cohort was categorised into three groups: the 23 chronic offenders (those who had received 6 or more convictions); the 109 non-chronic offenders and the remainder who were non-offenders. The factors that distinguished chronics from the non-chronics were, similarly, low family income, troublesomeness, low IQ, poor attainment at junior school and a convicted sibling. Each of these factors was present in about 60 per cent of the chronics compared with about 30 per cent of the non-chronics. These factors also discriminated the non-chronic offenders from the non-offenders.

Thus, by reference to the subject's early life, some factors can be used to identify a high-risk group of potentially persistent offenders. However, as these factors are broadly similar to those that distinguish all offenders from non-offenders, the difference being one of degree, the ability to predict subsequent persisting recidivists or chronics is limited. Developing a risk score, West classified 35 men as potentially persisting recidivists. Of this high-risk group about half (18) did become persisting recidivists. Of the remaining 362 men not in the high-risk group, 18 (5 per cent) became persisting recidivists. This result is fairly typical in prediction research (Farrington and Tarling, 1985). While it is possible to predict half of the persisting recidivists the other half will be missed, or alternatively, some (in this case about an equal number – 17) will be predicted to be persisting recidivists but will not in fact become so. (Prediction is discussed further in Chapter 9 in the context of incapacitation.)

The second approach, found most commonly in studies of recidivism, examines known offenders at some later point into their career, for example, when they are released from prison. (This approach is adopted in the next chapter.) The objective of these studies is to identify factors associated with an offender *continuing* a criminal career in the future. Because known offenders are included, information is available on the criminal career up to that point and this can be included in the analysis along with other background factors.

All studies of recidivism have found that the age of the offender and previous criminal history in particular (as measured by the number of previous arrests or the number of previous convictions) are the strongest factors associated with further offending. These findings are so universal that they require little elaboration here. Both are found to be important in the analyses reported in Chapters 6 and 7. It was also shown in Chapter 4 that the likelihood of a further conviction increased with the number of previous convictions, at least in the earlier stages of a criminal career. Other factors, such as age at first conviction or the most serious previous sentence, have also been found to be important, but in such cases they are usually acting as a proxy for previous criminal career.

Drug use

In certain cases there is a direct causative relationship between drugs and crime: drug misuse is defined as a crime under the drug control legislation. To this extent drug misuse is similar to alcohol consumption, discussed earlier, in that some acts are crimes by definition. What is of interest here is whether drug dependence is a factor in causing other types of crime to be committed. Drug dependence can lead to crime in two ways. First, otherwise non-offenders may turn to crime because of drugs, and, second, offenders who take drugs (whether or not they became offenders because of drugs) may commit offences at a higher rate than similar offenders who do not take drugs. That there should be a connection between drugs and crime, it is hypothesised, is because drug offenders need to obtain large sums of money in order to support their habit. Thus if legal income is not available or sufficient (as is usually the case), the addict will have to turn to crime, and in particular acquisitive crime (burglary, theft of money or readily resaleable goods), to raise the additional money required.

This review will only consider the relationship between the use of heroin and criminal behaviour.

It is generally recognised by reviewers (see Mott, 1991) that until about 1980 there was little connection between heroin and crime. Studies of addicts (Mott, 1980) revealed that apart from drug offences, and allowing for their age and criminal histories before coming to notice as official addicts, they were no more likely to be convicted of offences than the general run of offenders. The major effect of heroin use on their criminal histories was an increase in the number of convictions for drug offences.

After 1980 the picture changed. All available indicators pointed to a considerable increase in the extent of heroin use, a new group of users and a much stronger link between heroin and crime. The increase was localised – some areas were affected much more than others and Parker and Newcombe (1987) describe the pattern in Wirral, Merseyside, one of the areas to experience an increase. From 1979 to 1985 heroin use increased dramatically in the Wirral. So, too, did crime which increased more than in the rest of Merseyside or in the country as a whole. The disproportionate rise in crime was almost exclusively due to rises in two acquisitive crimes, theft from motor vehicles and burglary. These results suggest that the heroin epidemic in the Wirral was related to the parallel rise in crime. To provide further information Parker and Newcombe studied a sample of 300 Wirral residents convicted of certain property crimes at courts in the area. This sample was cross referenced with a list of known problem drug users (mainly heroin users) compiled in previous research. Criminal history information was also available. Parker and Newcombe found that 55 per cent of those convicted of burglary, 33 per cent of those convicted of theft, 13 per cent of those convicted of taking a car and 5 per cent of those convicted of criminal damage were known drug users. With the exception of criminal damage, these rates are much higher than would be expected, given the number of offences and the number of known problem drug users.

Parker and Newcombe also considered the chronology of the crime–heroin relationship. Have heroin users turned to crime or have criminals turned to heroin? The sample of 300 could be split into 'user–offenders' and 'non-user–offenders'. The user–offenders had a higher rate of convictions for acquisitive crime than non–users during the 1981–85 period. Users had an average of 6 convictions between 1981–85 compared with 3.4 for non–users. The number of convictions for non–acquisitive crimes were broadly similar for the two groups.

The user–criminal group could be split further into those who committed a crime before using heroin and those who used heroin before committing crime. Parker and Newcombe found that about a third did not commit their first crime until after the age of 16 and hence after they became heroin users. They concluded that for this group heroin use led them to offend for the first time. For some of this group, no doubt, Parker and Newcombe are correct in inferring that heroin led to the onset of a criminal career, but probably not for all of them. It was shown in Chapter 3 and repeated earlier in this chapter that a considerable proportion of offenders are late comers to crime. Thus to find a high proportion of late starters in any sample of offenders, whether they take drugs or not, is not so remarkable. What undoubtedly follows from this research, however, is that heroin use leads offenders to commit acquisitive crimes (but not other types of crimes – except drug offences) at a much higher rate than otherwise would be the case.

Confirmation of this result is found in a later study of 46 London–based heroin users (Jarvis and Parker, 1989). Annual rates of offending were calculated for the period from first conviction to the time the offender began using heroin and for the period after the offender began using heroin. The yearly rate of convictions for all crimes was over twice as high when using heroin compared with the pre–heroin period.

Self–report studies of heroin misusers conducted in Wirral, London, Nottingham and Glasgow between 1984 and 1986 provide further evidence. These showed that, while a few claimed that they financed their heroin misuse solely from drug dealing, many said they did so by committing acquisitive offences, most often burglary, thefts and handling stolen goods (Parker and Newcombe, 1987; Bean and Wilkinson, 1988; Jarvis and Parker, 1989; Hammarsley *et. al*. 1990). Very few of those interviewed admitted to committing violent offences, although some of the Nottingham group said that they had used or threatened violence to collect payment for illicit drugs.

Desistance

Very little systematic research has been undertaken on the factors that lead offenders to terminate their careers. This is in sharp contrast to the amount of research effort that has been devoted to explaining why some people begin committing crimes in the first place. Of course recidivism studies which consider why some offenders reoffend also provide evidence on why some do not. If, for example, young offenders are more likely to reoffend, then, older offenders are less likely to reoffend. The difficulty of drawing inferences about desistance from these studies is that the follow up period is usually only two or three years which is too short to give grounds for confidence that an offender has finally terminated his or her career. It may simply be a temporary lull in a continuing criminal career. A much longer period of inactivity is needed before any reliable conclusions can be drawn. To study desistance a cohort needs to be followed up for a considerable length of time, or alternatively, a sample of older ex-offenders needs to be studied. To date most cohorts have only been followed up to, at most, the early thirties and few studies have examined in any detail what caused ex-offenders to terminate their careers.

Despite the paucity of research some suggestive findings have emerged. During interviews, some members of the London cohort (Knight and West, 1975) volunteered reasons for having given up delinquency. A major reason given by some was no longer associating with delinquent friends. This may in some cases have been a conscious decision simply to avoid getting into situations leading to crime, whereas in others it may have arisen because the offender moved away from the neighbourhood. Osborn (1980) examined the convictions of those members of the London cohort who had moved outside the London area and found that their level of criminal activity was significantly reduced once they had moved away compared with those who had remained in London.

Other significant life events, such as getting married, have been put forward as a reforming influence on offenders. The systematic research evidence, such as there is, is more equivocal. Osborn and West (1979) found evidence of this for some offenders, in particular, for those members of the London cohort who married later in life. For others, those who married early or who married delinquent wives, marriage had little effect and perhaps even exacerbated offending. As West (1982) points out marriage leads to competing pressures. Married men described their lifestyle as becoming more conformist yet they also experienced greater financial pressures (they had more financial commitments and more debts). Thus, whether marriage is a restraining influence depends on the quality of the relationship and the change it causes in other circumstances.

One or two ethnographic studies which involved interviewing older ex-offenders have been carried out in the U.S. The most important of these was conducted by Shover (1983) who interviewed 36 ex-offenders (average age 51) and asked them to explain why they had ended their involvement in crime. Several reasons emerged. Some had developed a critical and detached perspective of their criminal youth. 'Taking stock' they realised that crime had been an unproductive enterprise – a 'dead end'. While taking stock they became aware of time as a diminishing, exhaustible resource, the future became increasingly valuable and they did not want to spend any part of it in custody. Aspirations changed with age, the desire for material gain had weakened and 'contentment' and 'peace' became more important to them. Some men simply became tired and weary of continuous involvement with the criminal justice system. Other reasons cited were a satisfying relationship with a woman, and other aspects of a more conventional lifestyle such as an interesting job, religion or involvement in educational courses.

From this, albeit limited, evidence it seems that desistance can either occur when circumstances change, (disrupting former entrenched lifestyles) or, when reflecting on their past involvement in crime, offenders take a more rational decision to end their criminal career. The two are not mutually exclusive. Either can initiate desistance and each can reinforce the other.

6 SURVIVAL MODELS

The first section of this book (Chapters 2 to 5) presented and explained such data as are available from Criminal Statistics and other sources on patterns of offending, especially in England and Wales. The three chapters which follow consider and extend the application of statistical techniques to data on offending. Work of this nature has increased lately both to aid understanding of criminal behaviour and to test more accurately the effectiveness of interventions and policy initiatives. This chapter examines survival models.

Often in criminological applications the focus of interest is the occurrence (or not) of a single event, for example, recidivism or 'failure'. Maltz (1984) in his review lists the various definitions of recidivism or failure that have been adopted. Return to prison, reconviction, rearrest or parole revocation were the most popular amongst the studies he examined. A typical follow up period was one or two years. Whether or not a subject failed within the follow up period was recorded and this dichotomous measure has been used as the criterion of assessment.

Although the simple dichotomous measure is informative there are several difficulties and limitations associated with this. First, the criterion, whether or not someone fails, results in loss of information as it says nothing about the time to fail. Ignoring this dimension can obscure important inferences about the timing of failure. As Cox and Oakes (1984) point out, merely recording whether someone fails during a fixed period wastes information because it examines what is essentially only one point on the survival curve. The extent to which inferences can be missed by ignoring the distribution of time to fail was shown by Stollmack and Harris (1974). They compared two groups of offenders released from prison. One group, of 185, was released directly to parole, the other, of 211 offenders, was released via a half-way house. The proportions who failed after one year were not significantly different but the distribution of the time to failure was. More of the group released directly to parole failed earlier during the follow up period than those released via the half-way house.

A second problem arises when applying standard statistical techniques such as multiple or logistic regression as they are not valid when the data are censored – as is usually the case. The imposition of a fixed follow up period means that for some subjects the only information available is that the event (failure) has not occurred prior to the end ('censoring') point. For example, *Prison Statistics England and Wales 1989* records that 50 per cent of a sample of male prisoners discharged in 1986 were reconvicted within two years but others in the sample may have been reconvicted at some later date. There is evidence to supply this from Phillpotts and Lancucki's (1979) study. They followed up a sample of 5,000 offenders sentenced in 1971. After two years about 50 per cent were reconvicted, but after six years 71 per cent were reconvicted following a custodial sentence.

The proportion failing within the follow up period, such as the example of 71 per cent of prisoners reconvicted within six years, is often quoted as a failure rate. But, as Maltz (1984) points out, this is not a rate in the accepted sense of the term. The percentage failing within a particular period is just the fraction or proportion failing, a rate is time based (he gives the example of speed which is measured in miles per hour). The failure rate or hazard rate is central to survival models.

Survival models have been developed for applications where the dependent variable is the time interval to some event. These models have been applied extensively in medical research and engineering where the dependent variable might typically be the length of survival following treatment or the life of a particular component. Survival models, therefore, are appropriate for analogous applications in criminology where the dependent variable is, for example, the time interval to the commission of an offence following sentence or release from prison.

There is now a growing body of literature on the application of survival models in criminology since their introduction by Carr–Hill and Carr–Hill (1972). At first sight this literature seems daunting, if not confusing. However, as Schmidt and Witte (1988) clarify in their important review, these studies can be conveniently classified into two main groups representing the different developments in this area. First, there are those studies that have considered alternative parametric frequency distributions for the time to failure. Included within this group are those studies that have examined 'split population' models (discussed later). Their primary focus has been to identify which distribution fits the data best or is most appropriate for criminological applications. The second broad classification covers those studies that have examined explanatory variables or covariates. This group includes studies that have employed the non-parametric (or more accurately semi-parametric) Cox's proportional hazards model. Although studies in this latter group may have considered the suitability of alternative distributions too, the main interest was to identify the social and background factors associated with failure and the time to failure. No doubt the lack of readily available computer software has contributed to these two separate developments; the investment in time and effort necessary to pursue one course ruled out pursuing the other. This is changing as software is becoming available, but it is by no means straightforward to conduct all these analyses. Schmidt and Witte (1988) in their latest study were the first to draw on both strands of research, as does the research reported here.

Statistical methods

This section briefly outlines the main statistical concepts of survival models.

Consider the interval to failure (the survival time), t, as a random variable and having a cumulative distribution function F(t). F(t) is simply the proportion of the sample that fails at or before time t. (The survivor function S(t) is the proportion of the sample that has survived - not failed - at or before time t. The survivor function is thus 1 - F(t).) The probability distribution function f(t), is the proportion of the sample that fails at time t. The hazard rate h(t) is defined to be the number that fail at time t expressed as a proportion of those in the sample that have survived up to time t. Thus:–

$$h(t) = \frac{f(t)}{1-F(t)} \quad \text{or} \quad \frac{f(t)}{S(t)} \qquad \text{Eq. 6.1}$$

The log-likelihood function, used to obtain the maximum likelihood estimators of the model, is:–

$$\log L = \sum_{i=1}^{n} [y_i \log f(t_i) + (1 - y_i) \log(1 - F(T_i)] \qquad \text{Eq. 6.2}$$

where:

y_i is a dummy variable which takes the value 1 for those who fail and 0 for those who do not fail before the follow up period (the censoring point)

t_i is the time to failure for those who fail

T_i is the end of the follow up period (the censoring point) for those who do not fail.

In effect this means that those who fail contribute log $f(t_i)$ to the likelihood function whereas those who do not fail contribute $\log(1 - F(T_i))$.

For the various models examined in this chapter, different distributions for $f(t_i)$ and $F(T_i)$ will be included in Eq. 6.2 to obtain estimates of the parameters.

The data

The sample comprised 738 men released from prisons in England and Wales on parole licence. This sample forms a subset of the sample originally assembled by Ditchfield (1989) who was interested in examining the extent of reoffending by parolees while on parole licence. Further details of the selection of the sample were given in Chapter 1.

The parolee's post-release record of convictions was examined in order to determine whether or not he had been convicted of an offence after release from prison. Files were then examined to identify the exact day that the *offence* took place. Thus the dependent variable was the time in days from release from prison to the commission of an offence and *not* the date of conviction which was a good deal later in many cases.

Certain groups of offenders in the original sample were omitted from this analysis. Offenders serving sentences of less than 18 months were excluded as no background information on them is contained on the Parole Index. This group formed the majority of those excluded but others, such as those followed up for only a short period of time or where there was a significant amount of missing data, particularly on key variables, were also excluded.

All 738 offenders were followed up for a minimum period of 30 months and this became the censoring point for the subsequent analysis. The principal covariates contained on the Parole Index, and available for analysis, are listed below:-

* Type of offence committed which led to the sample prison sentence
* Age at conviction

* Age at first conviction
* Number of previous convictions
* Type of occupation
* Employment status at time of original conviction
* Marital status
* Living arrangements following release from prison
* Employment arrangements following release from prison
* Reconviction prediction score

Most of the above variables are self-explanatory except, perhaps, the last. The reconviction prediction score (RPS) is a simple points score, expressed as a percentage, indicating the probability of reconviction within two years following release from prison. It is a weighted sum of many criminal history and background variables (including those above) shown to be related to reconviction. Further details of its make-up are given in Nuttall (1977) and Ward (1987). It is analogous to the Salient Factor Score used by parole decision making bodies in the U.S.

Survival distributions

Before constructing survival models it is important to consider the nature of the underlying distributions. The three graphs, Figure 6.1, Figure 6.2 and Figure 6.3, show in turn the probability density function, f(t), the hazard rate, h(t), and the cumulative density function, F(t), for the survival times of the 738 parolees.

The decline in the proportion failing over time shown in Figure 6.1 is fairly common in criminological applications. It suggests that the chances of reoffending are greatest shortly after release from prison. However, this pattern is better assessed by considering the hazard as it depicts the number failing at any point as a proportion of those who have survived to that point in time. The hazard is shown in Figure 6.2 and for this sample it generally declines over time, although it seems to be fairly constant over the first 12 months, declining more rapidly thereafter. The shape of the hazard is extremely useful in guiding the choice amongst alternative distributions.

Figure 6.3 shows the cumulative distribution and shows the proportion of the sample that has failed at or before time t. As already stated, the cumulative distribution function is most often quoted in recidivism studies and for ease of reference, some summary statistics are shown in Table 6.1.

Figure 6.1
Probability density function

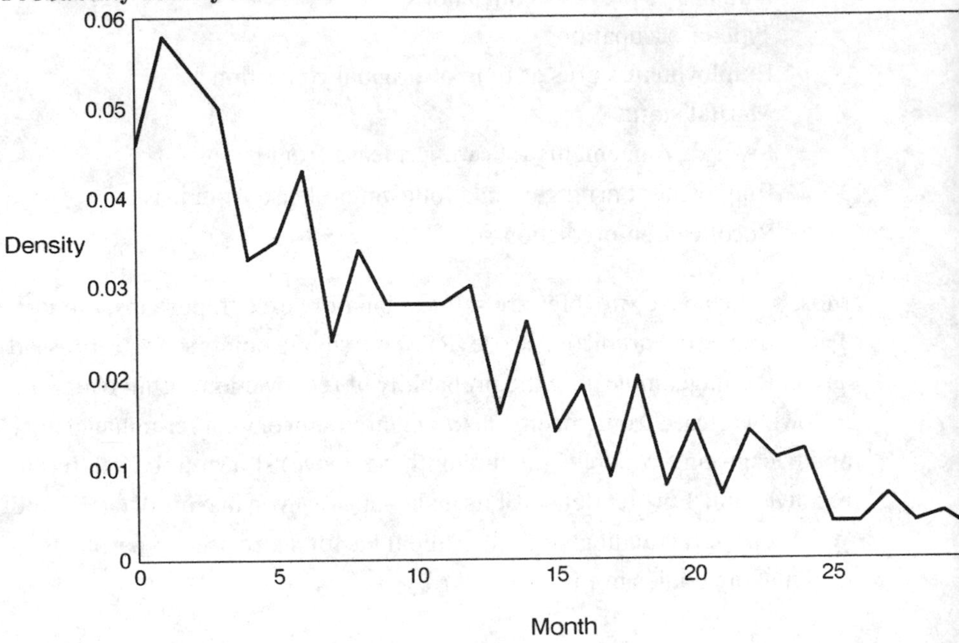

Figure 6.2
Hazard rate

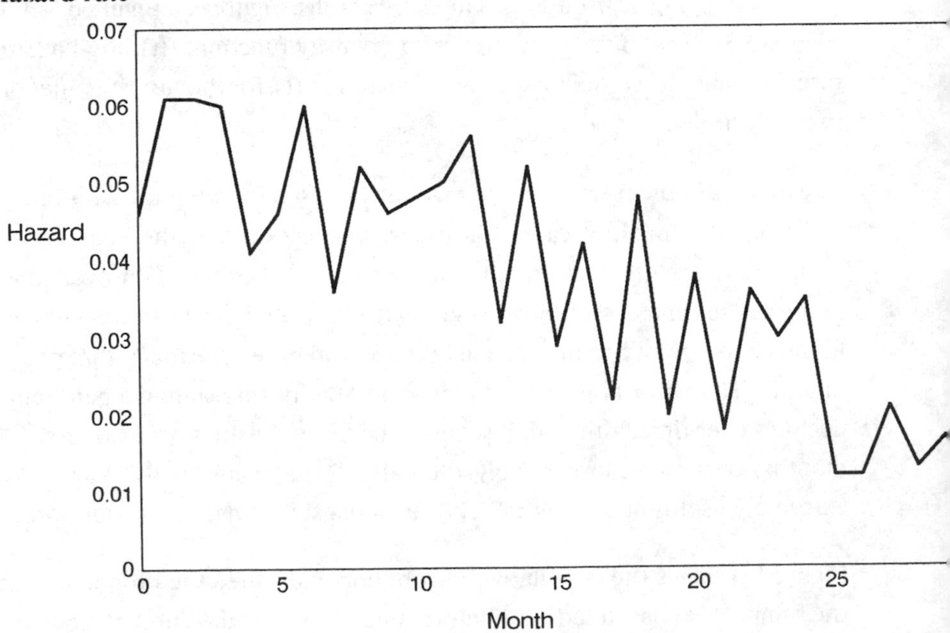

Figure 6.3
Cumulative density function

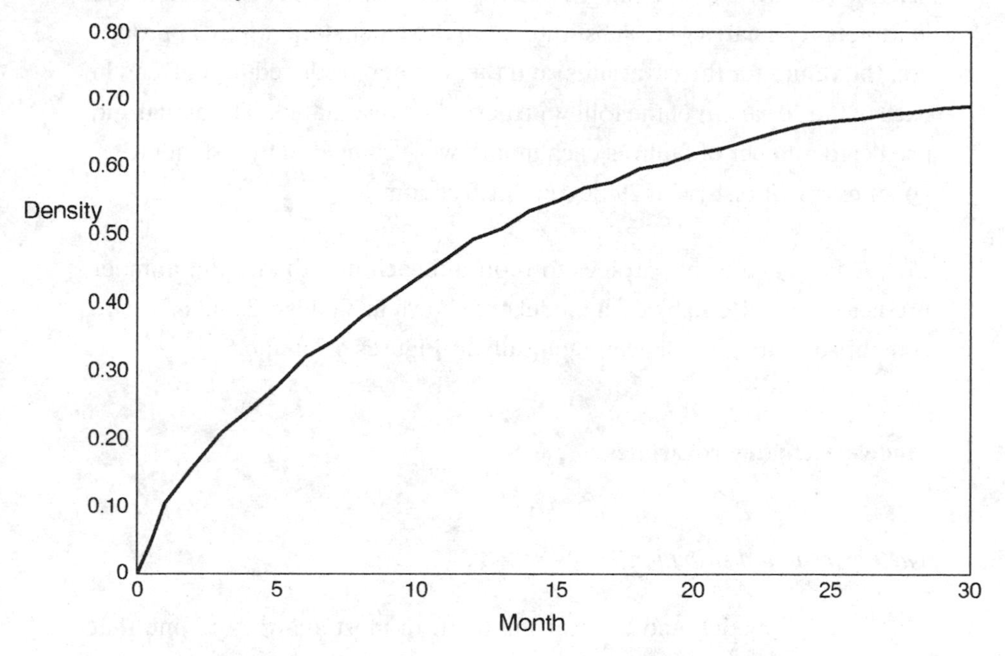

Table 6.1
Proportion of parolees reoffending within a given time period

Time (months)	*Percent failing*
6	28.3
12	46.9
18	57.9
24	65.9
30	69.1

Thus by the end of the follow up period (30 months) 69 per cent of the sample of parolees had committed a further offence.

Outline of analyses

Many models were developed and tested during the course of the analyses. Broadly, the approach taken was to consider various straightforward parametric models and then to consider split population models. In this first phase covariates were not included. The second stage was to conduct various analyses but on these occasions the covariates listed earlier were included.

The dependent variable in all analyses was the time to reoffend measured in *days*. However, to test the goodness of fit of each model developed, the parameter estimates were substituted into the model (and where appropriate, the values for the covariates) and the number predicted to reoffend in each of the 30 *months* of the follow up period was estimated. The actual and predicted number of failures each month were compared by a standard χ^2 goodness of fit test (with 29 degrees of freedom).

The actual number of parolees to reoffend each month and the number predicted to reoffend by each model are shown in Tables 6.2 and 6.3. The comparisons are also shown graphically in Figures 6.4 and 6.5.

Models excluding covariates

The exponential distribution

The simplest model, and the starting point in most analyses, is one that postulates 'time to failure' follows an exponential distribution. The exponential was first used by Stollmack and Harris (1974). It was also one of the models considered by Maltz (1984) and Schmidt and Witte (1988).

For the exponential:-

$$f(t) = \theta e^{-\theta t} \qquad \text{Eq. 6.3}$$

$$F(t) = 1 - e^{-\theta t} \qquad \text{Eq. 6.4}$$

$$h(t) = \theta \qquad \text{Eq. 6.5}$$

The attraction of the exponential is that it only has one parameter, θ, and has a simple explicit solution for the maximum likelihood estimator[6.1]. Note that the hazard for the exponential is constant, θ, which in this application means that a parolee's chance of reoffending is the same at all times following his release from prison.

For the sample of parolees, the maximum likelihood estimator for θ was found to be .00144. This value was substituted into (1 – F(t)) to produce the predicted number of offenders failing each month. These are listed in Table 6.2 and presented graphically in Figure 6.4. The χ^2 goodness of fit statistic,

Table 6.2
Number of parolees reoffending each month compared with numbers predicted to reoffend by the model: models without covariates.

*Month**	*Actual number of parolees reoffending*	*Number predicted by exponential without covariates*	*Number predicted by Weibull without covariates*	*Number predicted by split-exponential without covariates*
1	77	46.6	68.5	62.9
2	40	29.5	34.6	38.2
3	37	28.2	30.8	35.2
4	24	27.1	28.0	32.5
5	26	26.0	25.9	30.0
6	32	24.8	24.1	27.8
7	18	23.8	22.4	25.6
8	25	22.7	21.1	23.6
9	21	21.8	19.9	21.8
10	21	20.8	18.7	20.1
11	21	20.0	17.7	18.6
12	22	19.1	16.8	17.2
13	12	18.2	15.9	15.9
14	19	17.5	15.2	14.6
15	10	16.8	14.4	13.5
16	14	16.0	13.7	12.5
17	7	15.4	13.1	11.5
18	15	14.7	12.5	10.6
19	6	14.0	12.0	9.9
20	11	13.5	11.4	9.0
21	5	12.9	10.9	8.4
22	10	12.3	10.4	7.7
23	8	11.8	10.0	7.2
24	9	11.3	9.6	6.6
25	3	10.8	9.2	6.0
26	3	10.4	8.8	5.7
27	5	9.9	8.5	5.1
28	3	9.5	8.1	4.8
29	4	9.1	7.8	4.5
30	2	8.6	7.4	4.0
χ^2 goodness of fit Test comparing actual and predicted		$\chi^2 = 45.6$, $p < .05$, df = 29	$\chi^2 = 26.4$, not significant, df = 29	$\chi^2 = 14.8$, not significant, df = 29

* Given the way the months were calculated the first 'month' is, in effect, up to one and a half months.

Table 6.3
Number of parolees reoffending each month compared with numbers predicted to reoffend by the model: models with covariates

*Month**	*Actual number of parolees reoffending*	*Number predicted by exponential with covariates*	*Number predicted by Weibull with covariates*
1	77	55.4	65.8
2	40	34.1	36.3
3	37	31.8	32.7
4	24	29.7	29.9
5	26	27.9	27.5
6	32	26.1	25.4
7	18	24.5	23.6
8	25	23.0	22.0
9	21	21.5	20.5
10	21	20.3	19.2
11	21	19.1	17.9
12	22	18.0	16.9
13	12	16.9	15.8
14	19	16.0	14.9
15	10	15.1	14.1
16	14	14.2	13.3
17	7	13.5	12.5
18	15	12.7	11.9
19	6	12.0	11.2
20	11	11.5	10.7
21	5	10.8	10.0
22	10	10.2	9.6
23	8	9.8	9.1
24	9	9.2	8.7
25	3	8.8	8.2
26	3	8.4	7.9
27	5	7.9	7.5
28	3	7.6	7.1
29	4	7.2	6.8
30	2	6.9	6.5
χ^2 goodness of fit test comparing actual and predicted		$\chi^2 = 27.2$ not significant df = 29	$\chi^2 = 21.4$ not significant df = 29

* Given the way the months were calculated the first 'month' is, in effect, up to one and a half months.

Figure 6.4
Predicted and actual reoffending: models without covariates

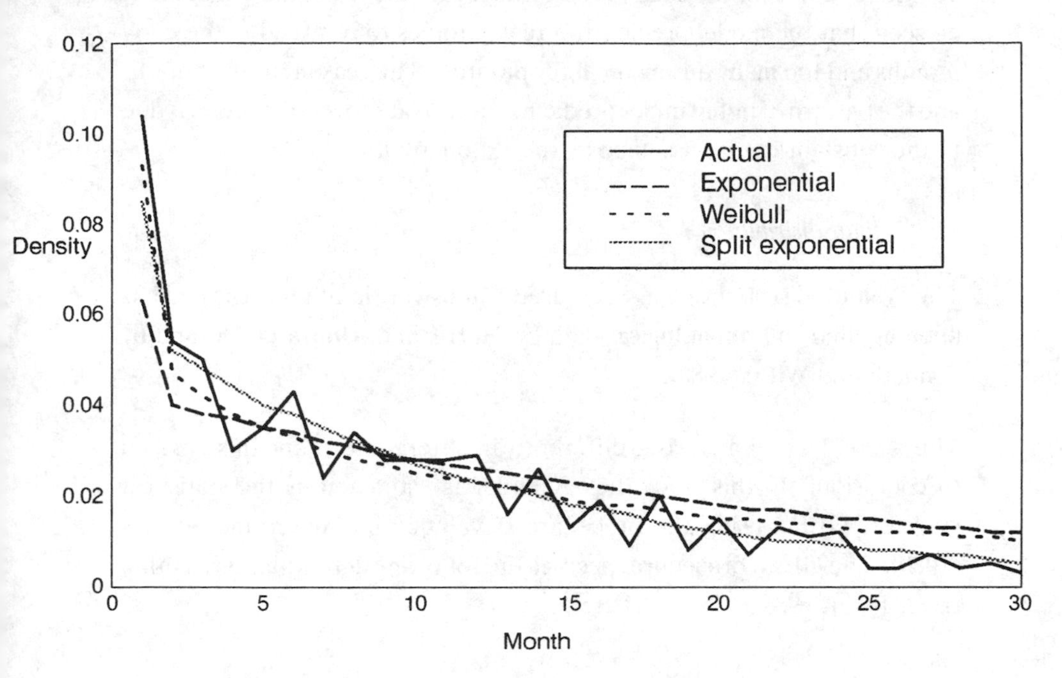

Figure 6.5
Predicted and actual offending: models with covariates

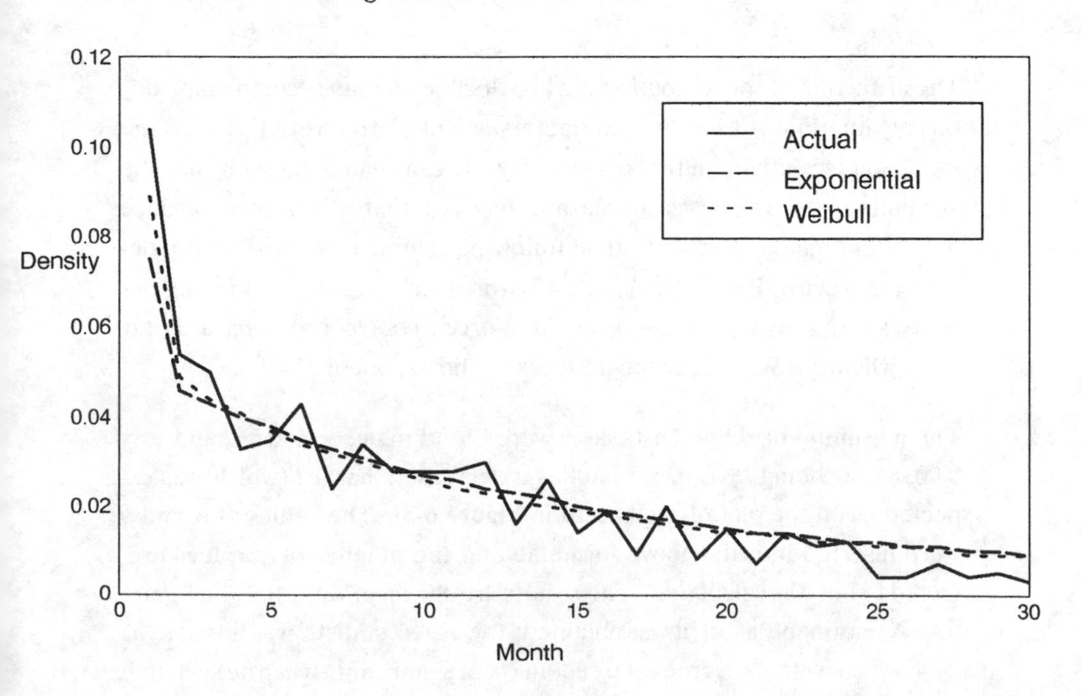

45.6, is significant at 5 per cent level indicating that the model is not adequate to represent the time to reoffend. From the table and graph it can be seen that the model predicts too few parolees to reoffend in the early months and too many during the later months. The reason for the poor fit and the pattern of initial under prediction and of later over prediction is due to the constant hazard assumed by the exponential.

The Weibull distribution

The Weibull distribution has been used extensively in other areas and has been applied to criminological data by Harris and Moitra (1978) and by Schmidt and Witte (1988).

The Weibull is parameterised differently in different texts and this can lead to confusion. In this study the Weibull was estimated by the statistical package, GLIM using the procedure developed by Aitkin and Francis (1980). The GLIM procedure specifies the following definitions (see Aitkin *et. al.* 1989)[6.2]:–

$$f(t) = \alpha\gamma t^{\alpha-1} e^{-\gamma t^{\alpha}} \qquad \text{Eq. 6.6}$$

$$F(t) = 1 - e^{-\gamma t^{\alpha}} \qquad \text{Eq. 6.7}$$

$$h(t) = \alpha\gamma t^{\alpha-1} \qquad \text{Eq. 6.8}$$

The attraction of the Weibull is that it is flexible and can accommodate different situations. It has two parameters α and γ often referred to as the shape and scale parameters respectively. It can readily be seen that the Weibull can have an increasing hazard (if $\alpha > 1$, that is, a parolee's chance of reoffending increases with time following release from prison) or a decreasing hazard (if $\alpha < 1$, that is, a parolee's chance of reoffending decreases with time following release from prison) or a constant hazard (if $\alpha = 1$) when the Weibull simply reduces to the exponential.

The maximum likelihood estimates were found to be, $\alpha = 0.847$ and $\gamma = 0.00384$. α being less than 1 implies a decreasing hazard (which was expected given the plot of the hazard in Figure 6.2). The values of α and γ were inserted into the above formulae and the number of parolees predicted to fail was calculated. The results are shown in Table 6.2 and Figure 6.4. A reasonably good fit was obtained; the χ^2 test statistic was found to be 26.4, which, with 29 degrees of freedom is not significant. It can be seen that the Weibull fits the data much better than the exponential, especially at the extremes of the distribution, that is, in the early months and in the later months following release. However, the error is still in the same direction as for the exponential. Both models predict too few reoffenders in the early months (3 to 4 months) and too many in the later months (from about 15 months onwards).

Split population models

An assumption in survival analysis, and with the models used so far, is that everyone is expected to reoffend given time. Under this assumption the fact that not everyone is observed to reoffend stems simply from the fact that each subject (in this case parolees) were only followed up for a fixed period of time. Many, however, criticise this conceptualisation and its applicability to criminal behaviour. While it may be perfectly valid to assume that every light bulb will eventually fail it is not the case that every offender will reoffend. It is well established that some will terminate their criminal career. A theoretically more appropriate model, therefore, is to postulate that a certain proportion will not reoffend but those that do reoffend will do so according to some survival (failure) process. Models that reflect this notion of two types of offender have come to be known as 'split population models'. Maltz and McCleary (1977) were the first to present and apply split population models in criminology but Schmidt and Witte's (1984 and 1988) clear description of these models is followed here.

Let F be an unobservable variable indicating whether an offender would or would not eventually fail. Specifically, let F = 1 for offenders who would eventually fail and δ for offenders who would never fail. Then assume:-

$$P(F = 1) = \delta, \; P(F = 0) = 1 - \delta$$

The parameter δ is the proportion eventually reoffending and 1 - δ is the proportion ending their career. Further, assume some cumulative distribution function $G(t|F = 1)$ for offenders who ultimately fail, and let $g(t|F = 1)$ be the corresponding probability density function. Note that such a distribution is defined conditional on F = 1, and it is irrelevant for offenders for whom F = 0, that is, for those offenders who would never reoffend.

Now let T be the length of the follow up period, and let y be the observable dummy variable indicating whether or not an offender has reoffended by the end of the follow up period. Constructing a likelihood function for the sample; for the recidivists y = 1 and the failure time = t, and it is known that F = 1. The appropriate density function to enter into their likelihood function is therefore:

$$P(F = 1)g(t|F = 1) = \delta g(t|F = 1) \qquad \text{Eq. 6.9}$$

On the other hand, for the nonrecidivists in the sample, y = 0, and the probability of this event is:–

$$\begin{aligned} P(y = 0) &= P(F = 0) + P(F = 1)P(t > T|F = 1) \\ &= 1 - \delta + \delta[1 - G(T|F = 1)] \qquad \text{Eq. 6.10} \end{aligned}$$

The first term in Eq. 6.10 reflects the fact that some people will never reoffend, whereas the second term reflects the fact that some people will reoffend after the censoring point.

The likelihood is then made up of terms like Eq. 6.9 for recidivists and Eq. 6.10 for nonrecidivists (offenders who have not reoffended by the end of the follow up period). The log likelihood function is:–

$$\begin{aligned} \log L = \Sigma\{&y_i[\log \delta + \log g(t_i|F_i = 1)] \\ &+ (1 - y_i)\log[1 - \delta + \delta(1 - G(T_i|F_i = 1))]\} \qquad \text{Eq. 6.11} \end{aligned}$$

The calculation of the maximum likelihood estimates of δ and whatever parameters are in the cumulative distribution function G will generally require a numerical maximisation of the likelihood function.

In the description above it is assumed that there are two types of offender, one type that simply does not fail and another that fails eventually according to some distribution. However, it is possible to postulate more types of offender where each type fails, but at a different rate. Carr-Hill and Carr-Hill (1972), Harris *et. al.* (1981), Maltz (1984) and Barnett *et. al.* (1987) all considered such models.

Split exponential model

The split exponential model assumes that those who reoffend, or those who will eventually do so, reoffend according to an exponential distribution. The split exponential is the model favoured by Maltz (1984). f(t) and F(t) of Eq. 6.3 and 6.4 are substituted for g(t) and G(t) in Eq. 6.11. Maximising the likelihood (6.3) shown in Eq. 6.11 obtained the values, δ = .759 and

$\theta = 0.00264$. Thus the model predicted that 75.9 per cent of the parolees will eventually reoffend. As would be expected the constant hazard, θ, is somewhat higher than for the exponential model discussed earlier (where $\theta = .00144$) as here it relates only to those who eventually fail.

The probability that an observed survival time is less than or equal to t is:–

$$\delta(1 - e^{-\theta t}) \qquad \text{Eq. 6.12}$$

The number predicted to fail each month was estimated using the above formula by inserting the estimates of δ and θ. The results are shown in Table 6.2 and in Figure 6.4. It can be seen that the split exponential produces a good fit. The χ^2 goodness of fit statistic is 14.8, the lowest so far obtained and the graph confirms the adequacy of this model in predicting reoffending for this sample.

Split Weibull model

The split Weibull is analogous to the split exponential except that the Weibull distribution replaces the exponential. The split Weibull has, therefore, three parameters; α and γ from the Weibull and δ, the splitting parameter.

Estimating this model produced the following results; $\delta = .741$, $\alpha = 1.07$, $\gamma = .00277$. It can be seen that the split Weibull is very similar to the split exponential and that little is gained by specifying that those who fail do so according to a Weibull distribution. Note in particular that α is approximately equal to 1 which implies a constant hazard and hence an exponential distribution. Because of this, the value of γ for the Weibull is similar to θ for the split exponential (.00277 compared with .00264). The Weibull predicts that 74.1 per cent of the sample will eventually fail. Given the similarity between the two and the adequacy of the split exponential, the number of parolees predicted to reoffend by the split Weibull was not calculated.

Models with covariates

The models discussed so far have not included any of the covariates or explanatory variables available for this sample of parolees. The second phase of the analyses incorporated these factors. Three models were considered – Cox's proportional hazards model, the exponential and the Weibull.

Cox's proportional hazards model

Cox (1972) proposed the proportional hazards model which is a non–parametric model for analysing survival data. The advantage of this model (and non–parametric procedures generally) is that it alleviates the problem of knowing the underlying distribution and is therefore extremely flexible and suitable in a wide range of applications. It accommodates censored data and covariates which vary over time. It can be used to identify important covariates and was used here for that purpose, as a precursor to using parametric models. To illustrate the method, Barton and Turnbull (1979 and 1981) applied the proportional hazards model to rearrest data for samples of offenders from two institutions in Connecticut. It was also used by Schmidt and Witte (1988) and by Allison (1984).

In Cox's model the failure rate or hazard, h(t), at time t is related to the covariates as:–

$$h(t,x) = h_0(t)e^{x\beta} \qquad \text{Eq 6.13}$$

where:

$h_0(t)$	is an arbitary (and unknown) or baseline non–negative function of time.
x	is the vector of covariates
β	is the vector of coefficients.

The factor $e^{x\beta}$ is the risk associated with value x for the regression variables relative to a value x = 0. For example, if β_i is positive this indicates that an increase in x_i will increase the hazard rate and thus will decrease the length of time to reoffend.

A further advantage of this model, stated above, is that the relative risk can vary with the time to fail by allowing components of x to depend on time, that is, x = x(t). There were no time varying covariates in this study but Allison (1984) did include time dependent covariates in his analysis. Details of the procedures for estimating β are given in Cox (1975) and are outlined in Schmidt and Witte (1988). They are not given here.

The proportional hazards model (above) is for continuous time and, in theory, ties should not exist. However, in practice they often do, as failure times might be grouped (for example, offenders rearrested in each month). Various adaptations to the basic model have been proposed for grouped data and Barton and Turnbull compared three of them. They found that all three gave very similar results, suggesting that there is probably little to choose between them. In this study, time to reoffend was measured in days and thus ties were not a significant problem.

Log–likelihood ratio test statistics are used to test alternative models and hence the contribution of individual covariates or sets of covariates. (This is analagous to comparing different log–linear models).

The proportional hazards model was applied to the data in this study primarily to identify those covariates related to time to reoffend(6.4). Alternative sets of variables were included but only three were found to be significant: age at conviction, the number of previous convictions and the reconviction prediction score. The coefficients and t statistics are shown in Table 6.4.

Table 6.4
Estimates of the coefficients for three models: exponential, Weibull and proportional hazards

	Type of Model					
Covariates	*Exponential*		*Weibull*		*Proportional Hazards*	
	b	*t*	*b*	*t*	*b*	*t*
Age at conviction	–0.054	–6.1	–0.053	–5.9	–0.051	5.7
Number of previous convictions	0.043	3.7	0.042	3.6	0.041	3.5
Reconviction Prediction Score	0.024	6.5	0.023	6.3	0.022	6.1
Constant	–6.818	–22.3	–6.344	–20.7	–	–
Shape parameter γ	–		.926		–	

The results from the proportional hazards model were used as a benchmark to compare other models: the exponential with covariates and the Weibull with covariates.

The exponential with covariates

The exponential with covariates is an extension of the exponential discussed earlier. However, in this case, although each offender is assumed to have a constant hazard each individual's (constant) hazard will depend on his value of the covariates. The way GLIM parameterises the model an individual hazard, θ_i, is equal to:–

$$\theta_i = e^{\Sigma x_i \beta_i} \qquad \text{Eq. 6.14}$$

However, GLIM estimates:–

$$\log \theta_i = \Sigma x_i \beta_i \qquad \text{Eq. 6.15}$$

Several models were estimated and the reduced model including the three important covariates is shown in Table 6.4. It can be seen that the three important variables are the same as those identified by the proportional hazards model: age at conviction, number of previous convictions and reconviction prediction score. The values of the coefficients were also very similar.

Interpreting the coefficients is similar to interpreting regression coefficients. The coefficient of –0.054 for age at conviction means that each additional year of age at conviction reduces the log of the hazard by 0.054, after controlling for other variables. An alternative is, $e^{-0.054} = 0.947$ which means that for each additional year of age at conviction the hazard is multiplied by 0.947. Thus the older the offender is at the time of conviction the less likely that he will reoffend. The effect of the other two covariates is in the other direction, in that the greater the number of previous convictions or the larger the value of the reconviction prediction score the greater the hazard and the more likely it is that the offender will reoffend. Considering first the number of previous convictions, $e^{0.043} = 1.044$, implying that with each additional previous conviction the hazard is increased by an estimated 4.4 per cent. Similarly for the reconviction prediction score $e^{0.024} = 1.024$, which implies that each unit increase in the score the hazard is increased by 2.4 per cent. Each offender's hazard was calculated by:–

$$\begin{aligned} \theta_i = \exp(-6.818 \; & - .054 \times \text{age at conviction} \\ & + .043 \times \text{number of previous convictions} \\ & + .024 \times \text{reconviction prediction score}) \end{aligned} \qquad \text{Eq. 6.16}$$

The probability that each individual would reoffend within a given time t was calculated. These probabilities were summed over all parolees in the sample (738) giving a number expected to reoffend. The predicted values are given in Table 6.3 and are shown graphically in Figure 6.5. It can be seen that this model produced a better fit than the exponential without covariates. The χ^2 goodness of fit test statistic was 27.2 which was not statistically significant.

The Weibull with covariates

The Weibull model with covariates is a natural extension of the Weibull; in the same way that the exponential with covariates is an extension of the exponential (discussed above). Thus:–

$$\log \gamma_i = \Sigma x_i \beta_i \qquad \text{Eq. 6.17}$$

It can be seen from Table 6.4 that the Weibull with covariates is similar to the exponential with covariates. The same variables were found to be significant and their coefficients were almost identical, the main difference being in the constant term – the difference here reflecting the additional parameter (the shape parameter α). The shape parameter, α, of .926 is approximately equal to 1 suggesting that the Weibull is little improvement over the exponential with covariates. (α of .926 here is also much higher than the α of .847 for the Weibull without covariates). However, there is some improvement over the exponential with covariates as can be seen in Table 6.3 and Figure 6.5.

Thus the three models with covariates, the proportional hazards, the exponential and the Weibull produced almost identical results and there is, on this evidence, little to choose between them.

Choice of model

Various approaches and models were adopted in this chapter to analyse the time to reoffend for a sample of parolees. The choice of model must be guided by the nature of the underlying distributions. In this application the hazard was found to be decreasing which suggests that a model, such as the exponential without covariates, which assumes the hazard to be constant and the same for everyone, is not adequate. This was borne out by the results. The Weibull produced a better fit as it could accommodate a declining hazard.

Schmidt and Witte (1988) considered the exponential "because it is a common one [model]... and also because it is a good example of how misleading an inadequate model can be". To understand this sentiment it is necessary to appreciate the nature of their data. In a series of studies, culminating in their latest account (Schmidt and Witte, 1988), they have examined data for several samples of prisoners released from prisons in North Carolina. Their dependent variable was the time interval to return to prison for those who were returned to prison. The probability density function and the hazard first increased (for about 10 months) and decreased thereafter. Not surprisingly, therefore, models such as the exponential (with a constant hazard) or the Weibull (with a monotonic increasing or decreasing hazard) did not fit their data well. Naturally, they considered models such as the log–normal which can accommodate changes in the hazard of this kind. The reason why the hazard for their data first increased and then decreased may be due to their definition of the dependent variable, namely the time to return to prison. Many prisoners may have committed crimes shortly after release but were not returned to prison until some time later due to the delays in catching offenders and in completing criminal proceedings. Whatever the reasons for the shape of their hazard, Schmidt and Witte's study reinforces the point that the nature of the distributions will influence the choice and adequacy of the model. In the analyses reported in this chapter the dependent variable was the time interval to the actual date the offence occurred and therefore not affected by any intervening delay caused by criminal proceedings.

It may be premature to dismiss the exponential as readily as Schimdt and Witte have done. Returning to the analyses here the exponential with co-variates proved an adequate model although the Weibull with covariates proved rather better. This would seem to suggest that individuals may have a constant hazard (or not such a significantly decreasing one) but that each person's hazard depends on background factors, in this case the age at con-viction, the number of previous convictions and the reconviction prediction score. Thus the observed declining hazard and probability density function are due to a changing composition of the type of offender surviving; those with a greater propensity to reoffend will do so quickly, leaving, as time goes on, a higher proportion with a lower propensity to reoffend.

The split exponential model produced perhaps the best fit to the data. It was stated that split population models have an intuitive and theoretical appeal in that they do not assume every offender will reoffend, but rather that some, as is well known, will simply terminate their careers. The split exponential was favoured by Maltz (1984). Schmidt and Witte (1988) also considered split population models and found them to be amongst the best that they tried. The power of split models found by Schmidt and Witte may also be due to the nature of their data. In their study approximately 37 per cent of the samples were returned to prison. Thus an assumption that everyone fails eventually seems implausible for their data. In this study 69 per cent of parolees reoffended which makes the assumption that all will reoffend, although theoretically wrong, less extreme.

Split population models can also be extended to include covariates. Such models were considered by Schmidt and Witte and later by Rhodes (1989) who prefers the description 'desistance/rate models' which he feels is more accurate – some offenders end their careers and do not fail while some do fail at a particular rate. Split population models with covariates are potentially very useful in analysing criminal behaviour. Covariates that affect whether or not a person fails can be incorporated along with covariates that affect the rate at which people fail (for those who do fail). However, these models are computationally very difficult to handle. The problem arises because theory does not clearly differentiate variables which affect desistance from those which affect time to failure for those who fail. In addition, many criminological variables, such as the number of previous convictions, are related to both the probability not to reoffend (desist) and the time to reoffend for those who do so. Left to itself the estimation procedure has difficulty distinguishing between alternative models and often does not 'converge' on a solution. If it does it results in high standard errors. Both Schmidt and Witte and Rhodes experienced this problem. Rhodes offers one partial solution by imposing constraints on the variables and Linster and Patterson (1987), in their study, suggest an alternative formulation to counteract this problem.

The analysis reported in this chapter did not extend to split population models with covariates because a range of simpler models proved adequate.

7 Stochastic models

The previous chapter considered the theory and application of survival models to analyse the probability of, and the interval to, the *next* offence (or arrest or conviction). In the process it highlighted desistance, the fact that some offenders terminate their careers and do not go on to commit a further offence. This led to the development of split population models which incorporate a specific parameter to represent the probability of committing a further offence. The present chapter extends the focus of interest to the occurrence of *several* events during the course of time or during a criminal career. Various stochastic models are presented and discussed. Some of the models explicitly address the issue of career termination.

To date, rather less thought has been given to the application and development of stochastic models in criminology than to survival models where a fairly extensive literature has evolved. Early, exploratory, work was undertaken by Carr-Hill and Payne (1971). They discussed the various single parameter probability distributions that might be used to model criminal careers; including the poisson, binomial and the geometric (the latter was considered in Chapter 4). They applied these models to data on a sample of 319 male offenders. Information was available for each subject on the number of court appearances. Their simple models do not fit the data well essentially because they assume that the rate of offending λ is constant over time, that is, thoughout a career, and is constant for all offenders. It was shown in Chapter 4 that the first assumption may not be too far wrong but the second is incorrect because λ varies between offenders. It is not surprising therefore that models that do not confront the heterogeneity in λ will not be adequate. Carr-Hill and Payne went on to propose what they called a heterogeneous poisson distribution which allowed λ to vary across offenders. This model fitted the data better but was not, in their terms, "very good".

Point process models

Copas and Tarling (1988) provide a general framework for the kinds of models introduced by Carr-Hill and Payne which allows for λ to vary between individual offenders and over time within a criminal career. Covariates were also included. Their models are all within the general class of *nonhomogeneous poisson processes*. It is assumed that within a period of an individual's criminal career, the number of occurrences of an event (such as arrest or conviction) and the exact times at which these events occur are determined by a chance process. Explicitly, the chance that an event occurs in the small time interval from time t to time $t + dt$ is $\lambda(t)dt$ where $\lambda(t)$ is the underlying rate function. In practice, $\lambda(t)$ will depend on predictive factors x_1, x_2 ..., as well as on time t. Furthermore, the x's may vary over time. If the x's relate to individuals, then each individual criminal career can be given its own particular probabilistic specification. If the x's correspond merely to a broad classification of individuals, then the model serves to describe and contrast the behaviour of different groups of such individuals.

Although a wide variety of patterns of occurrence of events can be described, these models retain an important mathematical simplicity in that they belong to the class of "Markov processes". The essential property of a Markov process is that behaviour in different time periods is assumed to be independent. So, for example, a rise in the number of offences (convictions, etc.) is explained by a rise in the underlying rate function $\lambda(t)$ rather than by a statistical correlation in which the chance occurrence of one event "triggers off" the occurrence of others[7.1]. (Markov processes are discussed further in Chapter 8 in the context of offence specialisation.)

λ *constant over time but varying between offenders*

To simplify the discussion, first take the special case of the rate functions being constant over time but varying between offenders. This variation is attributable to the different characteristics of offenders, denoted by their values of the x's. For a given period of study, the number of events then has a Poisson distribution (hence the name "poisson process"), but the expected number of events will depend on the x's and so be different across individuals or groups. The simplest model would be to allow λ to be a linear function of x, say $\lambda = a + bx$. But this is inadmissible since, for example, if b is negative and x exceeds $-a/b$, the fitted value of λ is negative, which would be impossible. The problem is removed by a logarithmic transformation, to give:–

$$\log \lambda = \alpha + \beta_1 x_1 + \beta_2 x_2 + \ldots \qquad \text{Eq 7.1}$$

where the argument t has been suppressed owing to the assumed homogeneity over time. If p_1 is the probability of an event between time t and time t + dt where dt is small, then

$$\log p_1 = \log dt + \alpha + \beta_1 x_1 + \beta_2 x_2 \; ..... \qquad \text{Eq 7.2}$$

This is therefore a log–linear model by direct analogy with the usual log–linear model used for analysing categorical data.

λ varying over time but constant for all offenders

Next consider another special case that is, in a sense, opposite to the one just described, and suppose that the rate function varies over time but is the same across individuals (or within a group of individuals). Here, the number of events no longer has a poisson distribution, and their occurrence might become more frequent, or less frequent, during the course of a criminal career and zero when criminals end their careers.

A dying away in the rate of offending with time could be modelled by another log–linear model

$$\log \lambda(t) = \log \lambda_0 - \nu t \qquad \text{Eq 7.3}$$

for a suitable decay coefficient ν. Here the rate starts at λ_0 and eventually decays to zero. A more flexible model is

$$\log \lambda(t) = \log \lambda_\infty + \log (1 + \gamma e^{-\nu t}) \qquad \text{Eq 7.4}$$

which corresponds to a long–term base rate of λ_∞ and an initial rate of $\lambda_\infty(1 + \gamma)$ with a smooth transition from one to the other (the mathematical penalty is that the log–rate is no longer linear in t).

λ varying over time and between offenders

The more general point process model now follows by combining together the dependence of the rate function on both time and the various x's. The most direct generalisation is to allow λ_0 or λ_∞ to be given by a log–linear model on the x's, for instance, the model

$$\log \lambda(t) = \alpha + \beta_1 x_1 + \beta_2 x_2 + ... + \log (1 + \gamma e^{-\nu t}) \qquad \text{Eq 7.5}$$

Each individual (or group) follows the same *shape* of time profile, but the *size* of the rate at any point of time is governed by the log–linear dependence on the x's. If there is just a single covariate x, and x = 0 is taken as the 'base level' then subjects at this base level value of x will have a rate starting at $e^{\alpha}(1 + \gamma)$ at $t = 0$ and moving as t increases to a long-term residual rate of e^{α}, according to the curve

$$\lambda(t) = e^{\alpha}(1 + \gamma e^{-\nu t}) \qquad \text{Eq 7.6}$$

The starting and finishing rates, and the rate of exchange from one to the other, are dictated by the values of the parameters α, γ, and ν. For subjects at some other nonzero value of x, the curve for $\lambda(t)$ is simply scaled up or down by a factor $e^{\beta x}$, β being the parameter governing the importance of the covariate x. More generally, βx in the scaling factor is replaced by a weighted sum of several predictive or explanatory factors.

Choice of Model

Unfortunately, adequate criminal career data were not available to Copas and Tarling (1988) to explore the empirical validity of their models. However, information presented earlier in this report (notably in Chapter 4) and elsewhere by others makes possible some assessment of the alternative models. All studies of offending behaviour show that λ varies between offenders; some offend intermittently others more prolifically. The difference between offenders may well be attributable to their values of the covariates (x's) although at present these relationships are not clearly understood.

In contrast, all the evidence currently available and discussed in Chapter 4 suggests that λ may not vary substantially throughout an individual offender's criminal career. This would suggest that models which permit λ to vary throughout a career may not be necessary. However, the age-crime curves presented in Chapter 2 indicate that most known offenders are young. If λ is constant over time for active offenders and does not decline it suggests that reduction in known offending at older ages is due to the fact that many offenders terminate their careers early. Indeed many careers are of short duration. This implies that models of criminal careers should include estimates of the likelihood that an offender will desist or terminate his career. This conceptalisation is analogous to the split population models presented in the previous chapter.

Models incorporating career termination

Reasoning similar to that outlined above led Barnett *et. al.* (1987) to propose a model that included estimates of both variations in λ between offenders and variations in p, the probability that an offender terminates his career after the kth conviction. The model was developed to analyse convictions up to age 25 for the male offenders in the London cohort taken from the Cambridge Study of Delinquent Development. As information was only available on convictions for this cohort (not all offences committed) the model estimated μ (the rate of convictions) not λ. μ varied between offenders. The probability of terminating a career also varied from conviction to conviction. It was shown in Chapter 4 (Table 4.3) that the probability of committing a further offence increased with each conviction, at least for the first few convictions, thereafter the probability was found to be constant. (The probability of terminating a career is simply 1 – the probability of committing a further offence.)

Barnett *et. al.* posited two sub populations within the cohort; (1) the "frequents" with a higher rate of convictions μ_1 with an associated p_1, and, (2) the "occasionals" with a lower rate of convictions μ_2 and an associated p_2. Note that it is assumed that p_1 and p_2 are constant at each conviction and that if p_1 is less than p_2 the lower drop out rate at each successive conviction (or the higher continuance probability) stems from the fact that, as the number of convictions increases, the population of offenders still active contains a higher proportion of frequents. One further estimate is needed, the proportion who are frequents, denoted by γ.

The following values were obtained:

frequents $\mu_1 = 1.14$, $p_1 = .10$
occasionals $\mu_2 = .41$, $p_2 = .33$
and the proportion frequents, $\gamma = .43$

Various tests of the model indicated that these estimates provided a good fit and that the heterogeneous cohort of offenders could be adequately represented by two homogeneous populations.

Following their initial analysis, the cohort was followed up for a further five years, to age 30. In a subsequent paper, Barnett *et. al.* (1989) were able to carry out a prospective test of their model. The original model accurately predicted the number of offenders who received a further conviction between ages 25 and 30, the total number of convictions and the time intervals between convictions.

Dugdale (1989) approached the problem in a slightly different way when he analysed court appearances for members of the 1953 Research and

Statistics Department cohort[7.2]. Essentially, his method was to fit separate split population survival models at each court appearance. After preliminary inspection of the data he realised that the model to first court appearance needed to be treated rather differently. For those who received at least one court appearance a Weibull distribution (see Chapter 6) was assumed. The survival function was

$$S_1(t) = 1 - p_1 + p_1 e^{-a(t-k)^b} \qquad \text{Eq 7.7}$$

where $1 - p_1$ represents the probability of never appearing in court and the second term represents the probability of survival up to time t given an offender does appear in court. As the cohort included both males and females, sex was entered as a covariate which has the effect of producing separate estimates of p_1 and a for each group. The estimates of the parameters were found to be

k = 3055 days
b = 2
p_1 males = .31
p_1 females = .08
a males = 1.069×10^{-7}
a females = 0.650×10^{-7}

A person cannot be convicted before the age of criminal responsibility and k was included to reflect this. The value of 3055 days is approximately 8.4 years which is close to the age of criminal responsibility (8 years) pertaining at that time. The value of p_1 for males is close to the participation rate up to age 28 presented in Chapter 3. (Dugdale only had available for analysis the first version of the cohort data which followed members up to age 28.) However, the estimate of p_1 for females, at .08, was higher than the participation rate for females (up to age 28) given in Chapter 3[7.3]. The estimate of a is also very different for males and females, indicating that the rate at which male offenders first appear in court is almost twice that of female offenders.

For all court appearances after the first a split population model was proposed and one based on the exponential distribution was found to be adequate. Thus the survival function was

$$S_i(t) = 1 - p_i + p_i e^{-\mu_i t} \qquad \text{Eq 7.8}$$

Note that as the person is now an offender (he or she has already appeared in court and been convicted at least once), k is no longer required.

Unfortunately Dugdale does not present estimates for males and females separately, the only estimates given are for the entire sample and are thus not reported in any detail here. Nevertheless, he does point out that when sex is entered as a covariate it has no effect on μ_i and its effect on p_i is significant but much weaker than for p_1 (the participation rate). The results are in broad agreement with those given in Chapters 3 and 4 where it was shown that although fewer females participate in crime, those that do commit crime at a similar rate to male offenders.

For the entire sample, μ_i was generally found to be about .5 (that is one *court appearance* every other year). P_2 was estimated to be .48, p_3, .65 and p_4, p_5 ... were approximately equal to .93[7.4].

Model to include length of criminal careers[7.5]

An alternative specification to that of including the probability that an offender will terminate his career after a particular conviction, is to incorporate estimates of career length. In other words, criminal careers can be conceptualised as being of a certain duration with offenders differing in the length of time that they are criminally active. Throughout a career an offender commits offences according to some rate λ. A model incorporating career length is developed here.

Let t be the length of a criminal career and assume that t is selected from a distribution $f_\theta(t)$ with parameter θ. Within that time period – starting at t_0 – an offender commits m offences at times t_1, $t_2 \ldots t_m$. Note, t_m is the time to the last offence. A distinction has to be made between those offenders who do not commit any offences after t_0 (that is for them $m = 0$) and those who commit one or more offences after t_0 (that is for them $m > 0$).

Focusing only on the latter group, those who commit one or more offences after t_0, assuming that they commit offences at rate λ

$$P(m > 0 \mid t) = 1 - e^{-\lambda t} \qquad \text{Eq 7.9}$$

$$\text{Thus } P(m > 0) = \int_0^\infty (1 - e^{-\lambda t}) f_\theta(t)dt \qquad \text{Eq 7.10}$$

$$P(t_1, t_2 \ldots t_m \mid t) = \begin{cases} \lambda^m e^{-\lambda t} & \text{if } t_m < t \\ 0 & \text{if } t_m > t \end{cases} \qquad \text{Eq 7.11}$$

Thus $P(t_1, t_2 \ldots t_m) = \lambda^m \int_{t_m}^{\infty} e^{-\lambda t} f_\theta(t)dt$ Eq 7.12

$$P(t_1, t_2 \ldots t_m \mid m > 0) = \frac{\lambda^m \int_{t_m}^{\infty} e^{-\lambda t} f_\theta(t)dt}{1 - \int_0^{\infty} e^{-\lambda t} f_\theta(t)dt} \quad \text{Eq 7.13}$$

If there are n offenders with $m > 0$ and the ith offender commits m offences the likelihood function $L(\lambda,\theta)$ is

$$L(\lambda,\theta) = \frac{\lambda^{\Sigma m_i} \prod_{i=1}^{n} \int_{t_{m_i}}^{\infty} e^{-\lambda t} f_\theta(t)dt}{\left(1 - \int_0^{\infty} e^{-\lambda t} f_\theta(t)dt\right)^n} \quad \text{Eq 7.14}$$

$$f_\theta(t) = \theta e^{-\theta t} \quad \text{Eq 7.15}$$

Note that the average length of a criminal career is $1/\theta$.

Substituting for $f_\theta(t)$ in Eq 7.14, the likelihood reduces to

$$L(\lambda,\theta) = \theta^n \lambda^{\Sigma(m_i - 1)} e^{-(\lambda + \theta)\Sigma t_{m_i}} \quad \text{Eq 7.16}$$

or

$$\log L(\lambda,\theta) = n\log\theta - \theta\Sigma t_{m_i} + \Sigma(m_i - 1)\log\lambda - \lambda\Sigma t_{m_i} \quad \text{Eq 7.17}$$

which gives maximum likelihood estimates for λ and θ of

$$\lambda = \frac{\Sigma(m_i - 1)}{\Sigma t_{m_i}} \quad \text{Eq 7.18}$$

$$\theta = \frac{n}{\Sigma t_{m_i}} \quad \text{Eq 7.19}$$

From Eq 7.18 and Eq 7.19 it can be seen that the maximum likelihood estimators of λ and θ are functions of three simple and straightforward measures; the number of offenders, the number of subsequent offences that they commit and the time to the last offence.

Introducing covariates into the model

So far it has been assumed that λ and θ are constant. However, evidence presented in Chapter 4 showed that the rate of offending and the length of criminal careers varies between offenders. Thus the model needs to be extended to incorporate covariates which affect λ and θ. Covariates can be introduced by letting

$$\log \lambda_i = \alpha + \beta_1 x_{1i} + \beta_2 x_{2i} \; ..... \qquad \text{Eq 7.20}$$

and

$$\log \theta_i = \gamma + \delta_1 x_{1i} + \delta_2 x_{2i} \; ..... \qquad \text{Eq 7.21}$$

and substituting in Eq 7.17.

The log likelihood function conveniently separates into two parts

$$\log L(\lambda): \; \Sigma(m_i - 1)(\alpha + \beta_1 x_{1i} + ...) - \Sigma t_{m_i} e^{(\alpha + \beta_1 x_{1i} + ...)} \qquad \text{Eq 7.22}$$

$$\log L(\theta): \; \Sigma(\gamma + \delta_1 x_{1i} + ...) - \Sigma t_{m_i} e^{(\gamma + \delta_1 x_{1i} + ...)} \qquad \text{Eq 7.23}$$

Both λ_i and θ_i can be estimated independently of each other and the effects of x_i on each can be assessed. Furthermore, both can be fitted readily using the statistical package GLIM by the instructions

YVAR	Y	where $Y = (m_i - 1)$	for estimating effects on λ (i.e. Eq 7.22)
		and $Y = 1$	for estimating effects on θ (i.e. Eq 7.23)
OFFSET	LT	where $LT = \log t_{mi}$	
ERROR	P	(poisson)	
LINK	L	(log)	
FIT		(model specification)	

Application of the model

To examine its utility, the model described above was applied to offenders in the 1953 Research and Statistics Department cohort. One current concern in criminological research, and one that is attracting a good deal of policy interest, is the criminal behaviour of young adults, that is, offenders aged 17 to 21. In order to throw some light on this issue all offenders in the cohort who had a conviction at age 17 were extracted and their subsequent criminal histories analysed.

Thus in terms of the model, t_0 is taken to be 17. However, information on actual offences committed is not available for members of the cohort but only information on convictions and court appearances. As an offender can receive several convictions at any one court appearance m was taken to be the number of subsequent court appearances after age 17 occurring at times t_1, t_2 ... t_m. Thus t_m is the time from age 17 until the last recorded court appearance.

By conceptualising the problem in this way two covariates could be constructed; age at first court appearance prior to age 17 – although for some offenders the conviction at age 17 was their first – and previous criminal history prior to age 17.

Of the male offenders in the 1953 cohort, 1,657 appeared at court and were convicted at age 17. For 624 offenders this was their last court appearance, at least before age 31 (that is for them $m = 0$). The other 1,033 male offenders had subsequent court appearances recorded against them ($m > 0$). Table 7.1 presents summary statistics for the two groups.

It can be seen from Table 7.1 that the two groups differed significantly. The group of 624 male offenders with no subsequent court appearances had few previous court appearances; 74.2 per cent had no previous court appearances – in fact, they had only one court appearance throughout their criminal career (the court appearance at age 17). Very few had two or more previous court appearances. In contrast the 1,033 male offenders who had subsequent court appearances after age 17 were much more likely to have previous court appearances and to begin their careers earlier; 36.7 per cent had no previous court appearances. About 43 per cent had started their career before their fifteenth birthday.

Note that an offender who began his career at age 17 will have no previous court appearances. Thus, for both groups the number (and per cent) with no previous court appearances is the same as the number (and per cent) whose age at first court appearance was 17. In fact, the two covariates were highly correlated, $r = -0.8$, thus, the fewer the number of court appearances the more likely that the offender began his career later.

Table 7.1
Number and proportion of offenders, by age at first court appearance and number of previous court appearances

Covariate	*Offenders with no subsequent court appearances after age 17*		*Offenders with subsequent court appearances after age 17*	
	number	*per cent*	*number*	*per cent*
Age at first court appearance				
8–12	46	7.4	224	21.7
13	19	3.0	98	9.5
14	28	4.5	124	12.0
15	29	4.6	99	9.6
16	39	6.3	109	10.6
17	463	74.2	379	36.7
Total	624		1033	
Number of previous court appearances				
0	463	74.2	379	36.7
1	95	15.2	220	21.3
2	32	5.1	152	14.7
3	17	2.7	101	9.8
4	7	1.1	73	7.1
5 or more	10	11.6	108	10.5
Total	624		1033	

Model to discriminate those with from those without subsequent court appearances

For the entire group of 1,657 offenders a logistic model was fitted to discriminate betweeen those who were convicted and appeared at court after age 17 and those who were not. The dependent variable was a simple dichotomy; $y = 0$ for those with no subsequent court appearances and $y = 1$ for those with subsequent court appearances. The two covariates, age at first court appearance and number of previous court appearances, were included in the analysis which was undertaken using GLIM.

The two covariates could be considered as either interval scaled variables or as categorical variables (factors in GLIM terminology). Each analysis was replicated with the variables alternately specified. (When treated as categorical variables the categories (levels) were taken to be those shown in Table 7.1.) In practice both procedures led to the same inferences.

Each covariate was found to be significantly related to whether the offender had subsequent court appearances when included independently in the model. When age at first court appearance was added it resulted in a reduction in χ^2 of 189.3 with 1 degree of freedom (the variable being treated as an interval scaled variable). The number of previous court appearances was found to be even more significant, $\chi^2 = 247.1$ with 1 d.f. Similar results were obtained when the variables were treated as factors; both were significant, previous court appearances more so. Treating the covariates as factors it was found that for age at first court appearance only ages 16 and 17 were significant. All levels of previous court appearances (0, 1, 2....5 or more) were significant.

However, including both variables in the model did not significantly improve the fit obtained by including number of previous court appearances on its own. Age at first conviction was not found to be significant when both variables were included. This result is not surprising given the high correlation between the two covariates. In statistical terms they are said to be confounded; once the number of previous court appearances is included age at first conviction has little to offer by way of additional explanation. Not surprisingly, the interaction term contributed little when it was added.

The model including the covariate number of previous court appearances is given below

	coefficient	*standard error*	*t value*
constant	–0.088	0.064	–1.4
number of previous court appearances	0.636	0.051	12.5

It can be seen from the model that an additional previous court appearance increases the log–odds of appearing in court after age 17 by a factor of 0.636. alternatively the odds of appearing in court are increased by $e^{0.636} = 1.89$.

Model for those with subsequent court appearances

For the group of 1,033 offenders who had subsequent court appearances after age 17 the model developed earlier was applied to estimate λ and θ and the contribution of the covariates. When applying the model, the distribution $f_\theta(t)$ has to be specified and it was assumed that the length of a criminal career follows an exponential distribution. Some assessment of this assumption is needed. It can be shown that if the length of a criminal career is distributed exponentially then the number or proportion of offenders appearing at court at ages 18, 19 .... 31 is also distributed exponentially. The proportion of offenders appearing at ages 18, 19 .... 31 was plotted for this group of male offenders and the results are shown in Figure 7.1. It can be seen that the assumption of an exponential distribution seems plausible and adequate, if not perfect.

Figure 7.1

Proportion of offenders appearing at court at ages 18 to 31

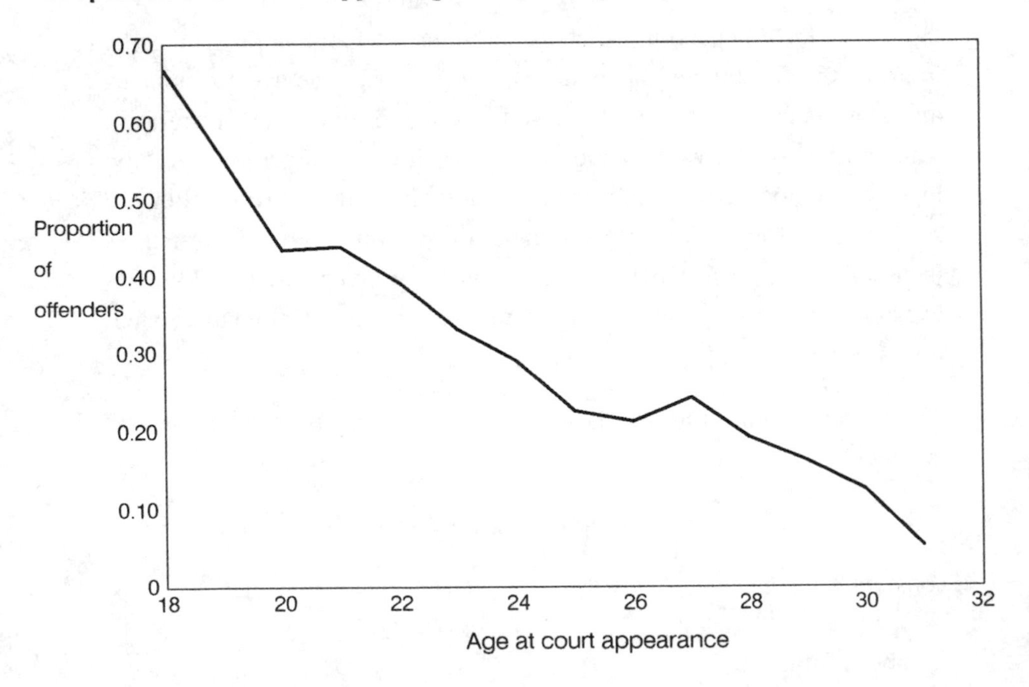

Given satisfaction with the credibility of the exponential, Eq 7.18 and Eq 7.19 were used to estimate λ and θ. For the entire group of 1,033 offenders the values were:–

$$\lambda = .446$$

$$\theta = .133$$

Thus after age 17, offenders appear at court, on average .446 times per year. The average length of a criminal career is $1/\theta = 7.5$ years. These results are comparable to those presented in Chapter 4 bearing in mind the different groups of offenders included in the various analyses.

Treating the covariates as categorical variables, their effect was assessed by calculating λ and θ for each level. The results are given in Table 7.2.

Table 7.2
Estimates of λ and θ for each level of the covariates

Covariate	λ	θ
Age at first court appearance		
8 - 12	.506	.115
13	.595	.134
14	.540	.118
15	.427	.152
16	.458	.145
17	.319	.143
Number of previous court appearances		
0	.319	.143
1	.415	.146
2	.429	.136
3	.597	.116
4	.595	.111
5 or more	.628	.109

Note that if an offender first appears at court at age 17 he will have no previous court appearances recorded against him. They are the same sub-group and hence the values of λ and θ are the same.

It can be seen that λ, the rate of subsequent court appearances, varies and generally declines with the age at first court appearance. Thus the later an offender begins his criminal career the lower his rate of subsequent offending. However, the number of previous court appearances has a more marked effect; the range of the coefficients is greater and the pattern more consistent. The larger the number of previous court appearances the greater is the rate of subsequent court appearances. It can be seen that offenders with no previous court appearances are likely to appear in court subsequently .319 times per year, whereas those with 5 or more court appearances are likely to appear in court twice as often (.628 times per year).

The two covariates are also related to θ (or the length of the subsequent criminal career $1/\theta$). However, the effect of age at first court appearance is less clear; again the effect of the number of previous court appearances is more marked and consistent. Each additional court appearance an offender receives before age 17 has the effect of reducing the value of θ (or increasing the length of his subsequent career). For those with no previous court appearances θ was found to be .143 or the length of the subsequent criminal career ($1/\theta$) to be 7 years; whereas those with 5 or more previous court appearances were estimated to have subsequent criminal careers of 9.2 years.

The significance of the two covariates can be assessed more formally by fitting the model in GLIM. The first to be examined was the effect of the covariates on λ, the rate of subsequent court appearances. Treating the covariates as interval scaled variables both age at first court appearance and number of previous court appearances were highly significantly related to λ when entered independently of each other (respectively $\chi^2 = 82.1$ and $\chi^2 = 204.2$ both with 1 d.f.). However, when entered together, age at first court appearance was only just significant at the 5 per cent level. When entered on its own the coefficient of age at first court appearance was negative suggesting that the younger the age at first court appearance the higher the rate of subsequent court appearances after age 17. However, after controlling for the number of previous court appearances the sign of the coefficient was positive. The coefficient of the number of previous court appearances was much greater and positive throughout as might be expected from Table 7.2. The model including both covariates considered as interval scaled variables is shown below.

	Coefficient	*Standard error*	*t value*
Constant	–1.339	0.157	– 8.53
Age at first court appearance	0.019	0.010	1.97
Number of previous court appearances	0.117	0.010	11.54

The weak relationship between age at first court appearance (after controlling for the number of previous court appearances) and the rate of offending is not surprising given the finding in Chapter 4 that μ is fairly constant and independent of the age at which a career begins.

Turning to θ, the effects of the covariates were much weaker than for λ. This is consistent with the estimates given in Table 7.2 where it can be seen that the range of the estimates for θ are less than those for λ. Both covariates were significantly related to θ, the number of previous court appearances slightly more so, although there was little to choose between them (for age at first court appearance χ^2 = 8.0, 1 d.f., for number of previous court appearances χ^2 10.6, 1 d.f.). When both covariates entered the model together the χ^2 of 10.9, 2 df was little or no better than for each of the covariates on its own. Although the combined effect of the two covariates was significant their joint presence resulted in neither attaining significance at the 5 per cent level. The model is given below.

	Coefficient	*Standard error*	*t value*
Constant	-2.097	0.311	-6.75
Age at first court appearance	0.010	0.019	0.54
Number of previous court appearances	-0.039	0.024	-1.68

The analysis suggests that neither covariate is particularly powerful in estimating or predicting the length of a subsequent criminal career.

8 OFFENCE SPECIALISATION AND MARKOV PROCESSES

Previous chapters considered the rate of offending and how this varies between offenders according to different characteristics. The scope is now extended to include the types of offences committed during the course of a criminal career. Two particular questions are examined. To what extent do the offences committed become less or more serious in the progression of a criminal career? Second, to what extent do offenders specialise in certain types of crime? A view frequently asserted about offending is that offenders begin their careers by committing trivial offences and escalate to more serious crimes later in life. On the other hand, another common assumption is that offenders specialise in the types of offence that they commit; offenders who commit burglary, for example, specialise in burglary and only very occasionally, if at all, commit other types of offence. The data available in this study enabled these assumptions to be explored empirically.

Crime switching: transition matrices

Wolfgang *et. al*. (1972) were the first to construct 'transition matrices' to assess specialisation in offending. Transition matrices show the probability of committing an offence of type j, having committed an offence of type i on the previous occasion. Hence, the probabilities p_{ij} indicate the chances of switching from one type of offence to another (offence i to offence j). The probability of committing the same type of offence on each occasion (p_{ii}, p_{jj} etc.) indicates the extent to which offenders specialise in their criminal behaviour. The degree of escalation or de-escalation in the seriousness of offending can be gauged by the probability of committing a more serious (or less serious) offence on subsequent occasions. Separate transition matrices can be constructed for successive offences: for example, a transition matrix can be constructed for the first offence to the second offence, from the second to the third offence and so on. Changes in these matrices can reflect the extent to which offending changes during the course of a criminal career. These ideas will become clearer later when data are presented. The general form of a transition matrix is set out in Figure 8.1

Figure 8.1
Transition matrix

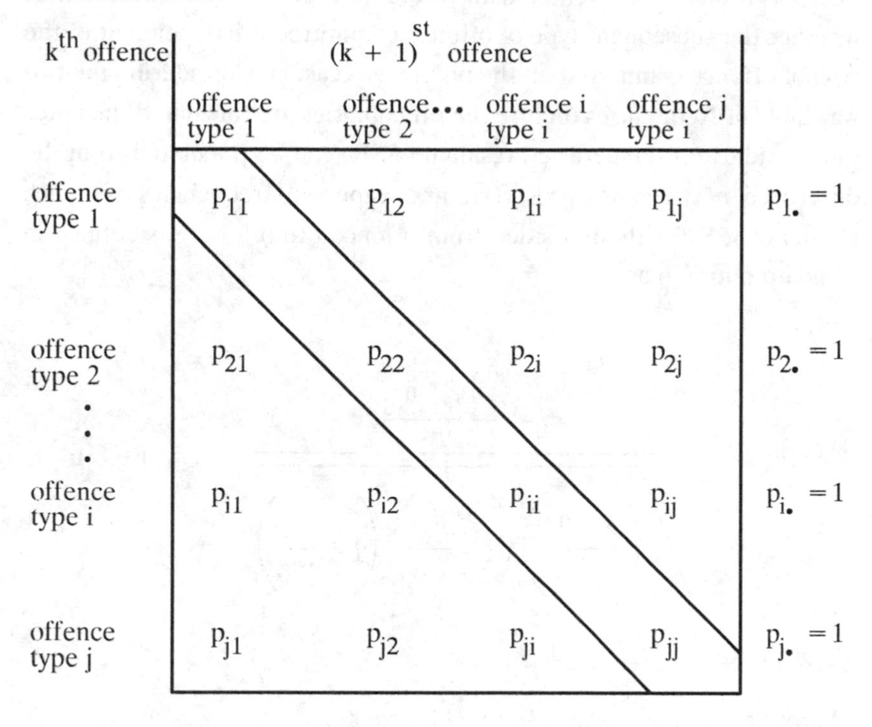

The elements in the matrix indicate the probability of committing a particular type of offence in relation to the type of offence committed on the previous occasion. The probabilities are calculated by simply dividing the frequency in each cell by the appropriate row marginal total ($n_{ij}/n_{i\cdot}$). The elements on the main diagonal (P_{11}, P_{22} .. P_{ii}, P_{jj}) are of particular importance as they are the probabilities of committing the same type of offence on both occasions and indicate the degree of specialisation in offending.

To some extent, however, probabilities will be dependent on the relative frequency of crime types. A common crime, such as theft, is likely to have a high probability of repetition irrespective of the previous crime committed whereas an infrequently committed crime may have an apparently low probability of repetition. Another point, rarely considered, is that diagonal probabilities, and hence the degree of specialisation observed, will also be influenced by the extent to which crime types are disaggregated. To give an absurd example by way of illustration, if all offences are put into one category 'crime' the diagonal probability will be 1. As crime is disaggregated into more and more crime types the probabilities are likely to get smaller.

Haberman (1979) provides a test statistic to test whether an element of the matrix is less than or greater than would be expected by chance, that is, whether the subsequent type of offence committed is independent of the type of offence committed on the previous occasion. Considering the two way table of frequencies (before the probabilities are calculated) he notes that an adjusted standardised residual (ASR) can be calculated from the difference between the observed and expected frequencies for each element. ASR for the transition from offence i to offence j is defined in standard notation as:–

$$ASR_{ij} = \frac{n_{ij} - \dfrac{n_{i.}\, n_{.j}}{n_{..}}}{\sqrt{\left(\dfrac{n_{i.}\, n_{.j}}{n_{..}}\right)\left(1 - \dfrac{n_{i.}}{n_{..}}\right)\left(1 - \dfrac{n_{.j}}{n_{..}}\right)}} \qquad \text{Eq 8.1}$$

where: n_{ij} is the observed frequency
$n_{i.}$ is the row marginal total
$n_{.j}$ is the column marginal total
$n_{..}$ is the grand total in the matrix

ASR is distributed as a standard normal deviate with mean 0 and variance 1, which permits a test of significance of the elements in the transition matrix.

An alternative way to test whether the elements on the main diagonal are greater than would be expected (and hence whether there is evidence of specialisation) is to fit a log-linear model to the data. A dichotomous variable indicating whether the cell is on the main diagonal or not is included. The influence of this variable on the overall fit of the model provides a test of specialisation. This model – the main diagonal model – has many applications in social science, for example, in voting behaviour studies where the interest is in whether people vote for the same political party at successive elections. It is described in detail by Fingleton (1984).

Farrington (1986) proposed the Forward Specialisation Coefficient (FSC) as an index of the degree of specialisation. As specialisation is referenced by the diagonal elements, FSC is only appropriate for these elements. FSC is defined as:-

$$FSC_{ij} = \frac{n_{ii} - \frac{n_{i.}\, n_{.j}}{n_{..}}}{n_{i.} - \frac{n_{i.}\, n_{.j}}{n_{..}}} \qquad \text{Eq 8.2}$$

FSC takes a value between 0 and 1. It is 0 when there is complete versatility in offending and 1 when there is complete specialisation.

Previous research calculating transition matrices

The methodology outlined above has been employed in a growing number of studies. Rather more studies have been carried out on samples of juveniles than adults and most of these have been undertaken in the United States. Few have included British offenders. Klein (1984) reviewed 33 studies of juvenile offending (mostly American) and concluded that there was virtually no evidence of specialisation; juveniles studied were versatile in their offence patterning. More recent studies of American juveniles (Bursik, 1980; Rojek and Erickson, 1982; Lab, 1984; Smith and Smith, 1984; Kempf, 1987; Farrington *et. al.*, 1988) modify that position, concluding "a small, but significant degree of specialisation superimposed on a great deal of versatility", (Farrington *et. al.*, 1988). Furthermore, most of these studies provide little evidence of escalation in offending; successive transition matrices were not significantly different from each other. The exception to this general pattern is Farrington *et. al.* (1988) who found some small evidence of escalation. Studies of adults in the United States found much stronger evidence of specialisation for all types of offence (Blumstein *et. al.*, 1988; Cohen, 1986). Although the dominant patten was one of similiarity between transitions matrices, Blumstein *et. al.* (1988) also found some evidence of escalation in seriousness of offending.

Earlier studies based on British samples indicated a good deal of versatility and little specialisation (West and Farrington, 1977; Walker *et. al.*, 1967; Soothill *et. al.*, 1976 and Mott, 1973). However, none presented transition matrices of the sort discussed above.

To date, three British studies have calculated transition matrices. Phillpotts and Lancucki (1979), in their study of 5,000 offenders convicted in January

1971, presented a matrix of transition probabilities from the type of offence committed in January 1971 to the type of offence on first reconviction for those males who were reconvicted. Their sample included male offenders of all ages. In contrast, the transition matrix produced by the Home Office Research and Statistics Department (1985) included only male juvenile offenders. In this analysis all three birth cohorts (1953, 1958, 1963) were combined. For those persons first convicted before the age of 16 and reconvicted within two years, the type of offence on first and second conviction was compared.(8.1)

The third study was conducted by Stander *et. al.* (1989) who analysed data for 698 male adult prisoners taken from the South East Prison Survey (described briefly in Chapter 4 and in more detail in Chapter 9). Unlike Phillpotts and Lancucki and the Home Office cohorts, Stander *et. al.* considered successive transition matrices, 10 in all, and having found them to be stationary (explained later) combined the matrices into one.

Table 8.1 presents evidence on specialisation provided by these three studies. The main diagonal probabilities are shown and for each the ASR was calculated to test the significance.

It is difficult to make direct comparisons between the studies as the classification of offences differs somewhat between them. Despite this it can be seen that there is clear evidence of specialisation; all probabilities are significant at the 1 per cent level. Thus the probability that an offender will commit the same type of offence next time is greater than chance. Having said that, the degree of specialisation is not particularly strong: only one probability is greater than 0.5; about half are 0.25 or less. The probabilities in the Stander *et. al.* study seem to be somewhat higher but this may be due to the fewer number of offence types.

Offenders who commit only one type of offence

Phillpotts and Lancucki approached specialisation from another angle and calculated the proportion of offenders who comitted only one type of offence throughout their career irrespective of what type that was. The results are presented in Table 8.2. The proportion of males with all offences of the same type was considerably smaller than that for females, regardless of the total number of convictions. This undoubtedly reflects the fact that theft offences predominate for females, much more so than for males (see Chapter 2).

Table 8.1
Diagonal transition probabilities from three studies

Type of offence	*Phillpotts & Lancucki*		*Home Office cohorts*		*Standen et. al.*	
	n	*p*	*n*	*p*	*n*	*p*
Violence against the person	211	.33**	1300	.08**	–	–
Violence against the person including robbery	–	–	–	–	253	.22**
Sexual offences	63	.22**	–	–	120	.50**
Burglary	–	–	–	–	1237	.41**
Burglary including robbery	551	.38**	16000	.43**	–	–
Theft and handling stolen goods	1018	.50**	17500	.45**	2437	.54**
Fraud and forgery	89	.21**	300	0	254	.31**
Malicious/ criminal damage	112	.11**	3500	.12**	–	–
Motoring offences[1]	113	.31**	3800	.22**	–	–
Summary offences	–	–	500	.10**	–	–
Other indictable offences[1]	55	.25**	500	.06**	650	.27**
Total number of transitions	2212		43400		4951	

** significant at 1 per cent level

(1) The category 'motoring offences' is not strictly comparable across studies. The Home Office Research and Statistics Department study included 'unauthorised taking or theft of a motor vehicle' in this category. The other two studies included these offences in the theft category. Similarly, the category 'other indictable offences' includes different offences in each study – being those offences not included elsewhere. n is the number of transitions.

Table 8.2
Persons convicted of standard list offences in January 1971 with two or more convictions for standard list offences in the period 1963 to 1976 whose convictions were all for offences of the same type, by sex and number of convictions

Number of convictions 1963–1976	*Total no. of persons*	*Persons with all convictions for offences of the same group*		
		Number	*% of total*	*% of total expected on 'chance' hypothesis*
Males				
2	684	318	46	28
3 to 5	1,133	184	16	7
6 or more	1,146	30	3	0.4
Total	2,963	532	18	9
Females				
2	103	70	68	62
3 to 5	76	28	37	41
6 or more	29	9	31	15
Total	208	107	51	48

The continuous decrease for both males and females in the observed proportions in Table 8.2 demonstrates that the more times an offender has been convicted previously, the less likely it is that the offences will all be of the same type. Phillpotts and Lancucki examined whether the proportions in Table 8.2 could occur by chance. The expected proportion of persons with all convictions of the same offence type was estimated and is also shown in Table 8.2. For males, the observed proportions were considerably higher than those expected and indicate that there is a tendency for males to stick to one offence type throughout their career. For females the observed and expected proportions were similar for those with fewer than six convictions. This may be explained not so much by a lack of any tendency to repeatedly commit similar offences as by the fact that a very high proportion of females are convicted of one type of offence; theft and handling stolen goods.

Further analysis of offence specialisation

To extend the evidence for this country on the degree of specialisation in criminal careers, analysis was undertaken on the sample of offenders convicted at the Crown Court. (The sample is described in Chapter 1.) The analysis was confined to males who had more than one court appearance. Thus, from the initial sample 226 females and 401 male first offenders were excluded leaving a sample of 1,450.

Parallel analyses were carried out on two sets of offence groupings. The first comprised ten mutually exclusive offence categories:

1 violence against the person
2 sexual offences
3 robbery
4 burglary
5 theft and handling stolen goods
6 fraud and forgery
7 criminal damage
8 drug offences
9 motoring offences
10 other offences.

Some of these categories were combined to form a reduced set of five offences:

I violence against the person and robbery
II sexual offences
III burglary
IV theft and fraud
V other (comprising criminal damage, drug offences, motoring and other from the first classification).

The first step was to decide which transitions to examine. Unlike Stander *et. al.*, Phillpotts and Lancucki and the Research and Statistics Department study only considered one transition matrix; from the first offence (or the offence that brought the person into the study) to the first reconviction (second offence). Thus neither provided any information on whether other transition matrices (for example, between the fourth and fifth offence) are the same as the first transition or on how transition matrices change during a career. In the analysis undertaken here the first twelve transition matrices were calculated and the next step was to test whether adjacent transitions were constant (or stationary).

Stationarity

Goodman (1962) proposed two simple methods, based on chi–square, to test whether transition matrices are stationary. The two methods reflect the two basic approaches; first, adjacent pairs of matrices (transitions) can be tested across all offence types, and second, all transitions can be tested within offence types. Both procedures were followed here.

As an example of the first procedure, consider the first adjacent pair of transitions from the first offence to the second and from the second to the third. Successive tables (one for each offence) can be drawn up with two rows. The first row indicates the type of offence leading to a conviction at a second court appearance, for those offenders convicted of offence type i at their first court appearance. This analysis was not undertaken for the full ten offence categories. There are five columns – one for each of the possible types of offence listed in the reduced set of offences. The second row indicates the offences committed which led to the conviction at the third court appearance for those offenders convicted of type i offences on their second appearance in court. Thus a 2 x 5 table is constructed and a χ^2 statistic (with 4 degrees of freedom) can be calculated in the usual way. This procedure of drawing up 2 x 5 tables and calculating χ^2 can be repeated for each of the five separate offence types. The 5 χ^2 values can be added to produce a test statistic (with 20 degrees of freedom) for the entire transition across all offences. This was undertaken and the results are shown in Table 8.3.

With 20 degrees of freedom a χ^2 of 31.4 would be needed to obtain a significance of 5 per cent. Hence, it can be seen from Table 8.3 that only one (transition 9,10 compared with 10,11) of the χ^2 statistics was significant, indicating that in the main adjacent transitions were not different from each other.

Table 8.3
Comparison of adjacent transition matrices across all 5 offence types

Transitions			χ^2	*df*
1,2	compared with	2,3	18.9	20
2,3	"	3,4	22.2	20
3,4	"	4,5	16.6	20
4,5	"	5,6	11.3	20
5,6	"	6,7	19.8	20
6,7	"	7,8	24.3	20
7,8	"	8,9	25.0	20
8,9	"	9,10	19.7	20
9,10	"	10,11	33.4	20 $p < .05$
10,11	"	11,12	24.5	20
11,12	"	12,13	22.1	20

Confirmation of this result was sought by employing the second procedure. In this analysis a separate matrix was constructed for each offence type, the twelve rows representing the number of offenders convicted of that offence at first, second, ... twelfth court appearance. The columns indicate the types of offence committed at the second, third ... thirteenth court appearance. The analysis was undertaken first using the ten offence categories resulting in a 12 by 10 table (with 99 degrees of freedom) and repeated using the five offence categories resulting in a 12 by 5 table (with 44 degrees of freedom). The results are shown in Table 8.4

Two of the fifteen comparisons attained statistical significance at the 5 per cent level. They were criminal damage in the first classification and, in the second, theft, handling and fraud and forgery. Inevitably the numbers in some of the matrices (especially for the less frequent offences at the later transitions) are small and χ^2 tests should be treated with caution. Nevertheless, taken together, and in the light of the results in Table 8.3, there is no general evidence that transition matrices are different. It can be concluded that they are stationary (constant). This result is in line with that obtained by Stander *et. al.* (1989) who also found their transition matrices to be stationary. Thus the probability of offence j being preceded by offence i was no different on the thirteenth court appearance than the second court appearance nor on any of the intervening court appearances.

Table 8.4
Comparison of twelve transitions within each offence

Type of offence	χ^2	*df*	
Violence against the person	118.8	99	
Sexual offences	104.6	99	
Robbery	101.4	99	
Burglary	118.3	99	
Theft and handling stolen goods	104.1	99	
Fraud and forgery	103.7	99	
Criminal damage	131.6	99	$p < 0.5$
Drugs	97.9	99	
Motoring	114.7	99	
Other offences	96.0	99	
Violence against the person and robbery	54.7	44	
Sexual offences	35.9	44	
Burglary	33.2	44	
Theft, handling stolen goods, fraud and forgery	62.9	44	$p < 0.5$
Criminal damage, drugs, motoring and other offences	29.6	44	

Transitions from one offence to another

On the basis that the transitions from one offence to another are stationary the 12 transitions can be pooled to provide information on the probability of committing a certain type of offence, having previously committed an offence of a certain type. The pooled results are shown in Table 8.5 and Table 8.6 for first ten then five offence categories.

Table 8.5
Transition matrix: probability of committing offence type j having previously committed offence type i, 10 offence types

Court appearance *k*		*Court appearance k+1* *V*	*S*	*R*	*B*	*T*	*F*	*C*	*D*	*M*	*O*
Violence against the person (V)	(689)	.24** (+)	.02	.02	.19	.26* (–)	.03	.08** (+)	.03* (+)	.03	.11** (+)
Sexual offences (S)	(112)	.05	.25** (+)	.02	.19	.27	.11** (+)	.02	.01	.02	.07
Robbery (R)	(130)	.17** (+)	.02	.09** (+)	.21	.32	.03	.06	.01	0	.12
Burglary (B)	(2578)	.06* (–)	.01	.02	.43** (+)	.32* (+)	.02* (–)	.04	.01* (–)	.02	.08
Theft and handling stolen goods (T)	(3200)	.08	.01	.02	.28** (+)	.40** (+)	.04	.04	.02	.03	.08* (–)
Fraud and forgery (F)	(258)	.06	.05** (+)	.03	.17* (–)	.40	.12** (+)	.02	.03	.02	.10
Criminal damage (C)	(444)	.12* (+)	.01	.01	.27	.32	.03	.09** (+)	.03	.03	.10
Drugs (D)	(128)	.07	.02	.02	.18	.27	.06	.03	.26** (+)	.03	.08
Motoring (M)	(242)	.08	.01	.01	.16	.30	.06** (+)	.04	.01	.24** (+)	.09
Other (O)	(771)	.13* (+)	.01	.03	.21** (–)	.32	.04	.05	.03* (+)	.04* (+)	.14** (+)

* $p < .05$
** $p < .01$
Number of transitions is given in brackets

Table 8.6
Transition matrix: probability of committng offence type j having previously committed offence type i, 5 offence types

Court appearance k		*Court appearance k+1*				
		VR	*S*	*B*	*TF*	*O*
Violence against the person and robbery (VR)	(819)	.26** (+)	.02	.19* (-)	.30* (-)	.24** (+)
Sexual offences (S)	(112)	.07	.25** (+)	.19	.38	.12
Burglary (B)	(2578)	.08	.01	.43** (+)	.34* (+)	.14
Theft, handling stolen goods, fraud and forgery (TF)	(3458)	.10	.02	.27	.45** (+)	.16
Criminal damage, drugs, motoring and other offences (O)	(1585)	.14** (+)	.01	.21	.35	.29** (+)

* $p < .05$
** $p < .01$
Number of transitions is given in brackets

It can be seen from Tables 8.5 and 8.6 that there is evidence of specialisation. ASRs were calculated for each of the elements on the main diagonal and were found to be significant at the 1 per cent level. In addition a log–linear model was fitted to each of the frequency tables which formed the basis of Tables 8.5 and 8.6. A dichotomous variable representing the diagonal elements was included and found to be highly significant in both cases. (For the ten offence categories shown in Table 8.5, the diagonal term reduced χ^2 by 502.6 for 1 d.f. and for the five offence categories shown in Table 8.6, the diagonal term reduced χ^2 by 451.0 for 1 d.f.). However, and in line with other studies of this sort, the probabilities on the main diagonal are not particularly high. Only the probabilities for burglary and theft attain 0.4 or above. For many offences in Table 8.5, robbery, fraud, criminal damage and other, the probability does not reach 0.2. The elements on the main diagonal in Table 8.6 are the same or higher (never less) than the elements on the main diagonal in Table 8.5. This highlights the point made earlier that the size of the probabilities depend, to some extent, on the degree to which offence categories are disaggregated. Amalgamating many offence categories, each reflecting a small degree of specialisation, will increase the value of the probability of repeating that, more aggregated category of offence.

So far interest has focussed on the degree of specialisation and has thus concentrated on the main diagonal elements. But if offenders do not commit the same offence again what offences do they commit? Are there typologies or clusters of offences that different offenders specialise in? The off–diagonal elements in the matrices provide the answer although there are methodological issues to take into account. Considering each of the rows in both tables it can be seen that after the main diagonal elements the highest probability was for theft and handling stolen goods. Burglary was also prominent. But these results reflect the relative frequency of theft and burglary offences. In addition, significantly higher than expected probabilities on the main diagonal will themselves depress the size of the off–diagonal elements. As a result, tests of significance – such as calculating ASRs – may lead to the false conclusion that those who commit offence i are less likely than expected to commit offence j next time[8.2].

A more appropriate way to analyse the data is to eliminate the main diagonal elements from the table and approach the issue from the viewpoint 'what offences do offenders commit next time if they *do not* commit the same offence again?' This procedure was followed here and the standardised residuals were estimated after the main diagonal elements were omitted[8.3]. The off–diagonal elements that were significant from this analysis are indicated in the Tables. A + sign indicates that the offender was more likely to commit the offence than expected and a – sign indicates that the offender was less likely to commit this offence than expected.

From the results in Tables 8.5 and 8.6 certain patterns emerge. The clearest pattern seems to be burglary and theft which are positively associated in that offenders who commit theft (burglary) are more likely to commit burglary (theft) next time if they do not commit theft (burglary) again. Thus there appears to be a group of property offences that offenders specialise in – although interestingly this does not include fraud or robbery. The other patterns are less pronounced although there appears to be a cluster of violence related offences; violence, robbery and criminal damage, and these offenders are somewhat less likely to commit property offences. Curiously, sexual offences and fraud appear positively related but it is difficult to offer an explanation. Drugs and motoring offences seem to be more independent offences in that offenders who commit either are not more or less likely to commit any other specific type of offence. The category 'other' is a mixture of many offences and despite its relation to certain types of offence not too much can be made of the results.

Despite the interesting patterns revealed in the tables the overwhelming conclusion remains that while there is evidence of a small degree of offence specialisation the picture is one of great variety and versatility in offending.

Markov processes

Several of the studies referred to above examined whether criminal careers conform to a Markov process (Wolfgang *et. al.*, 1972; Smith and Smith, 1984 and Stander *et. al.*, 1989). A Markov process assumes that future states (in this application the type of offences committed) are determined by the current type of offence committed and the number (r) of previous types of offence committed. The *first order* Markov process is the simplest. Here it is assumed that the next type of offence committed is dependent on the current type of offence committed, but is not dependent on the types of previous offences committed. The first order Markov process is 'memory-less' in that knowledge of the previous types of offences committed in a criminal career is not helpful in predicting the next type of offence. Only knowledge of the current type of offence is useful for that purpose. Or, as it is often stated, given the present, the future is independent of the past. Markov processes can, of course, be of any order. An rth order Markov process assumes that the next type of offence is dependent on the current type of offence and the past r–1 types of offence.

A Markov process is said to be stationary if the probability of committing a certain type of offence in the future, is the same throughout a career. A first order Markov process that is stationary can be characterised by a single matrix of transition probabilities.

A first order Markov process, particularly one that is stationary, has important substantive implications and has several advantages for analysing criminal careers. If, indeed, offending does follow a first order Markov process it implies that an offender who has committed many previous offences of, say, burglary, is no more likely to commit an offence of burglary in the future than a person who has the same current offence but who has not previously committed an offence of burglary. Only the type of current offence would determine the future types of offence committed. First order Markov processes have other attractions including the possibility and the simplicity of making certain predictions: for example, the probability that an offender will at some stage in his career commit an offence of a certain type; the expected number of successive offences of a certain type; and, the likely number of offences of each type given a certain number of future offences. It is useful, therefore, to examine whether offending does, indeed, conform to a Markov process.

Wolfgang *et. al*., 1972, concluded from analyses of the Philadelphia cohort that a stationary first order Markov process was adequate to represent their data and this result provided impetus for future research. But, reassessing their results, Cohen (1986) points out that the χ^2 value obtained by Wolfgang *et. al*. was significant at the 7 per cent level, which she felt, provided some evidence for rejecting the first order Markov process. Stander *et. al*. (1989), recalculated χ^2 and suggested that Wolfgang *et. al*. under-estimated it by a slight amount but sufficient to produce a value that would have led them to reject the hypothesis even at the 5 per cent level. On their own data Stander *et. al*. firmly rejected the first order Markov process.

A further examination of the issue was undertaken here by analysing the sample of offenders sentenced at the Crown Court. It has already been demonstrated above that transition probabilities for this sample are stationary. The analysis was extended to test the assumption of the first order property. The procedure followed was the simple method proposed by Goodman (1962). His method requires the data to be arranged in a three way table as depicted below.

Table 8.7
Table for testing whether offending is a first, rather than second, order process.

Type of offence at t–1	Type of offence at t	Type of offence at t + 1		
		Offence 1	Offence 2. . .	Offence i. . .
Offence 1	Offence 1	offence 111		
Offence 2	Offence 1			
•	•			
•	•			
Offence i	Offence 1			offence i1i
•	•			

Similar tables are constructed with offence 2 at time t, offence 3 at time t, ... offence i at time t .... and so on. The cells of the tables contain the number of offenders with that combination of type of offence on the three successive occasions. χ^2 can be calculated for each separate table and the χ^2s summed to provide an overall value. The χ^2s provide a test of whether the transition probabilities depend on the offences committed on the two previous occasions (t–1 and t) or only on the type of offence committed at the immediately preceding period (t). The overall χ^2 value indicates whether the process is first order or not and the individual χ^2s for each table provide a test for each type of offence at time t.

The results of this analysis are presented in Table 8.8. Given the large number of cells in a three way table compared with the amount of data available, the analysis was confined to the five aggregate offence groups.

Table 8.8
χ^2 values to test whether offending is a first order markov process

	χ^2	*df*
Violence against the person and robbery	64.16**	16
Sexual offences	31.73*	16
Burglary	139.02**	16
Theft, handling stolen goods, fraud and forgery	337.41**	16
Criminal damage, drugs, motoring and other offences	137.24**	16
Total	709.56**	80

* $p < .05$
** $p < .01$

It can be seen from the results presented in Table 8.8 that the hypothesis that offending is a first order Markov process can be firmly rejected. All the χ^2 statistics were significant, mostly at the 1 per cent level. It is clear that the type of offence that an offender commits is dependent on previous criminal history and not just on the type of offence committed on the previous occasion. Unfortunately, it was not possible here to extend the analysis to test the exact order of the process.

Nevertheless, rejecting the first order property has important implications in stating that knowledge of the types of offence committed in the past, together with knowledge of the current offence category, provides a pointer to the type of offence likely to be committed on the next and subsequent occasions.

9 INCAPACITATION EFFECTS OF CUSTODY

It is hoped that the data presented on offending so far in this study have an intrinsic value but the findings presented are also of great interest in that they enable us to make calculations about the incapacitation effect of imprisonment. Indeed this controversial topic has been one of the main reasons for developing work on patterns of offending behaviour. In this chapter earlier work on estimating the incapacitation effect of prison will be reviewed. The lessons drawn will be used to estimate the possible effects of incapacitation on crime in England and Wales.

Obviously, while offenders are in custody they cannot commit crimes in the community. By taking people out of circulation, prisons do at least have some preventative function; while they are locked up, prisoners are effectively prevented from carrying out those crimes they would otherwise be free to commit.

In assessing incapacitative effects three questions can be posed. First, how many crimes are prevented by current or past levels of imprisonment? Second, what would be the effects on the levels of crime if the use of imprisonment was increased or decreased? And, third, can imprisonment be used in a more specific or selected way to control levels of crime? All three questions have been addressed by research, if not fully answered. Each is considered here in turn.

The effect of current levels of imprisonment

Much of the earlier research on incapacitation emanates from the United States and attempted to estimate the amount of crime averted by custodial sentences. These earlier studies are also important as they set out the various methodological approaches to measuring incapacitation effects. They are, therefore, discussed in some detail.

Using data on the Philadelphia Birth Cohort (Wolfgang *et. al.*, 1972), Clarke (1975) estimated the increase in the amount of crime if no juvenile had been incarcerated. The cohort comprised 9,945 boys born in 1945. By their eighteenth birthday 13.6 per cent of them had been arrested for an index offence, (non-negligent homicide, rape, robbery, burglary, grand larceny, and auto-theft) but only 381 boys had ever been in custody during this period. Estimating that the boys in the cohort committed at most 1.3 index offences per year, Clarke calculated that if none had been incarcerated, the total crime committed by the cohort would have increased by 5 to 15 per cent. Knowing that approximately one half of persons arrested were juveniles and assuming that their chance of being arrested was about twice that of adults, Clarke estimated that 28 per cent of reported index offences were committed by juveniles and thereby concluded that only 1 to 4 per cent of all index crimes were avoided by the incapacitation of juveniles.

Using FBI criminal careers data for 1965, Greenberg (1975) estimated that offenders committed between 0.5 and 3.3 offences per year. From these estimates and adopting other assumptions (about the proportion of crimes reported to the police and the proportion of persons arrested who were arrested for the first time – 'virgin arrests') he deduced that if prisons were eliminated entirely, index crimes would increase by between 1.2 per cent and 8 per cent. (Greenberg's method is not discussed in any detail here).

To measure the number of crimes prevented by incapacitation Avi-Itzhak and Shinnar (1973) and Shinnar and Shinnar (1975) proposed a rigorously derived model which has been adopted and adapted in much subsequent study. Their model is:-

$$I = \frac{\lambda qJS \left(\frac{T_R}{T_R + S} \right)}{1 + \lambda qJS \left(\frac{T_R}{T_R + S} \right)} \qquad \text{Eq 9.1}$$

Many of the terms in the model were defined in Chapter 1 and discussed in Chapter 4 but for ease of reference they are defined again here.

λ is the rate at which offenders commit crimes (see Chapters 4 and 7)

q is the probability of being apprehended, cautioned or convicted for a crime

J is the probability of being sentenced to imprisonment having been convicted

S is the average time spent in custody

qJS is therefore the expected time spent in prison for a crime.

T_R is the average residual career length

$\left(\frac{T_R}{T_R + S}\right)$ reflects the likelihood that an offender is still active after serving a sentence.

$\left(\frac{S}{T_R + S}\right)$ is the probability that an offender's criminal career ends T_R while he is still in custody.

If T_R is large compared with S, $\left(\frac{T_R}{T_R + S}\right) \rightarrow 1$, and equation 9.1 reduces to:–

$$I = \frac{\lambda qJS}{1 + \lambda qJS} \qquad \text{Eq 9.2}$$

Shinnar and Shinnar (1975) employed their simplified model (Eq 9.2) to analyse New York crime data. Substituting values for the parameters, qJS, assuming offenders commit between 6 and 14 crimes per year and inserting the average value of $\lambda = 10$ they estimated that incapacitation had the actual effect of reducing crime in 1970 by 20 per cent from its potential level.

Research evidence is also available from Sweden. Sjoberg (1978) applied the Shinnar and Shinnar model (Eq 9.2) to Swedish data and found for 1976, that the incapacitation effect in that country was no greater than 10 per cent and probably a good deal less. His estimate was derived using the maximum value of $\lambda = 21.7$ (based on the assumption that all known crimes were committed by convicted offenders – see Chapter 4 for the application of this approach to data for England and Wales).

Peterson and Braiker (1980) interviewed 624 inmates in Californian prisons in 1976 and asked them to state the crimes they had committed during the three years preceding their term of imprisonment. From the responses, estimates of λ could be derived. Multipling λ by the prison population and by making assumptions about the proportion of crimes reported to the police and so on, Peterson and Braiker calculated the number of crimes prevented compared to the number committed. The incapacitation effect was 22 per cent for armed robbery, 6 per cent for burglary and 7 per cent for auto-theft.

It can be seen that although there is general agreement that the proportion of potential crimes prevented by the level of custodial sentences prevailing at the times of studies is relatively modest, the authors disagree as to its actual value. Estimates of the incapacitation effect that existed at the time of the studies range from up to 4 per cent (Clarke), up to 8 per cent (Greenberg), not more than 10 per cent (Sjoberg) to 20 per cent (Shinnar and Shinnar, Peterson and Braiker).

Cohen (1978, 1983) critically assessed the earlier U.S. studies. Firstly, she notes, the principal discrepancy between them can be attributed to the assumption each has made about the rate at which offenders commit crime, λ. Clarke estimated that the boys in his study committed at most 1.3 index offences per year. Greenberg estimated that offenders commit up to 3.3 offences per year, whereas Shinnar and Shinnar put this figure between 6 and 14 crimes per year.

Cohen suggests that both Clarke and Greenberg's estimates of the rate at which individuals commit crime are too low which, consequently, led them to underestimate incapacitation effects. Clarke assumes all the juvenile offenders in the cohort are criminally active between the ages of 7 and 17. This is obviously not the case. Some offenders start their criminal careers later than others and some desist before age 17. Hence not all careers span 10 years and the effect of shorter careers would be to increase the rate λ, and hence the incapacitation effect. Greenberg's estimates, on the other hand, are based on his assumptions about the rate at which offences are reported to the police and the proportion of all persons arrested who are arrested for the first time. Cohen shows that relatively small changes in these two proportions, which are, *a priori*, equally plausible to those adopted by Greenberg, increase the rate at which offenders commit crimes from 3.3 to 6.3 per year.

Subsequent U.S. research (Blumstein *et. al*. 1986 – discussed in Chapter 4) suggests that the average value of λ in that country is between 9 and 13.

Another criticism can be levelled against Shinnar and Shinnar's study – namely, their use of the simplified model (Eq 9.2). This model assumes that offenders, if free, would commit crimes at the same rate. It does not take into account that some offenders will terminate their careers in prison. (Studies of recidivism, discussed earlier, show that some offenders do not reoffend when released from prison.) The application of Eq 9.2 will therefore overestimate the effects of imprisonment in reducing crime. This can be verified by using the full model Eq 9.1. Keeping the parameter values the same as those used by Shinnar and Shinnar and setting T_R at 10 years reduces the incapacitation effect from 20 to 16 per cent. If T_R is reduced to 5 years the incapacitation effect falls to 13 per cent. The estimates obtained by Peterson and Braiker may also be too high due to the unrepresentativeness of the prisoners interviewed (the prisoners interviewed were thought to have higher λ's than other prisoners).

These studies differ in other respects which may contribute to the different estimates obtained. For example, Clarke only considered juveniles; the location of the studies varied: Philadelphia (Clarke), national data, (Greenberg), New York (Shinnar and Shinnar) and California (Peterson and Braiker). Given the different crime rates and different uses of imprisonment, it is likely that incapacitation effects will be different too.

Although the estimates are generally modest there are grounds for thinking that they are still too high. The fact that some offenders terminate their careers while in custody has already been noted. However, a further reduction is necessary because some offences are committed by several offenders. For example, if two offenders together commit the same crime, incarcerating both offenders beforehand would only have prevented one crime. Some adjustment downwards is therefore needed to avoid double counting. The adjustment needed will depend on the distribution of crimes committed by more than one offender. In Chapter 5 it was shown that the average number of offenders per crime was between 1.5 and 1.7.

Other issues need to be borne in mind. Incapacitating some types of offenders will not necessarily reduce particular crimes to the same extent. An example here is the sale of drugs. Imprisoning a drug dealer may not reduce drug dealing if another dealer simply takes over the market left by the one imprisoned. The level of drug offences is more likely to be determined by the demand for drugs than the supply of them. (Wagstaff and Maynard, 1988, discuss this and other economic aspects of the illicit drug market.)

These earlier studies are important in that they generated an interest in incapacitation and set out the many methodological approaches and the problems encountered when trying to measure the effects of custodial sentences. The lessons learned can be applied when estimating incapacitation effects in this country.

The incapacitation effect in England and Wales

It has been argued that Shinnar and Shinnar's full model, Eq. 9.1, is the most suitable to estimate the effect of custodial sentences in reducing crime in this country. Before applying the model to British data, estimates are needed for each of the key parameters; s, the average time spent in custody, qJ, the probability of being apprehended, convicted and given a custodial sentence, T_R, the residual career length and λ, the rate of offending.

Estimating S and qJ

Special analysis of the Prison Index, kindly undertaken by the Research and Statistics Department of the Home Office, provided information on the average time spent in custody, S, by those discharged in 1975, 1980 and 1986. Time in custody, including time on remand and under sentence, were provided for each major category of offence which led to the custodial sentence. This information is presented in Table 9.1.

Table 9.1
Average time in years spent in custody, S, by those discharged from custody; 1975, 1980 and 1986, by offence.

	Average time in custody, S		
Offence	*1975*	*1980*	*1986*
Violence against the person	.874	.693	.671
Sexual offences	1.227	1.260	1.063
Burglary	.745	.512	.605
Robbery	1.619	1.332	1.353
Theft/fraud and forgery	.578	.422	.416
Total (including. other offences)	.696	.532	.562

qJ is the probability of being sentenced to custody for a crime and is estimated as the number of people sentenced to custody as a proportion of the number of known offences. For 1975, 1980 and 1986, qJ was estimated to be:–

1975 qJ = .024
1980 qJ = .025
1986 qJ = .019

Estimating T_R

T_R can be estimated if certain assumptions are made. If the length of a career is distributed exponentially with mean residual career length T_R and if time served in prison is also exponentially distributed with mean length S (both assumptions seem reasonably plausible) then $T_R/(T_R + S)$ is the probability (P_A) that an offender is still active in a career after serving a sentence. Thus:–

$$\frac{T_R}{T_R + S} = P_A$$

$$T_R = \frac{P_A S}{(1 - P_A)} \qquad \text{Eq 9.3}$$

Recidivism data provides estimates of the probability P_A. Phillpotts and Lancucki (1979) followed up for a period of six years a sample of 5,000 offenders sentenced at court in January 1971. About fifty per cent of the sample were reconvicted within six years but reconviction rates varied according to sex, age, type of offence committed and the type of sentence awarded. They found that 71 per cent of those released from custodial sentences were reconvicted. Furthermore, for young adult males with 5 or more previous convictions who were released from custody the percentage reconvicted reached the high 80s. These results are in accord with those presented in Chapter 4 where it was shown that after obtaining four convictions the probability of receiving a fifth was about .8. As the majority of prisoners have 4 or more convictions (see the data for parolees in Table 4.1), P_A can be assumed to be .8.

Substituting in Eq. 9.3 the values of P_A and S given in table 9.1, the following estimates of T_R were obtained.

$$1975\ T_R = 2.8 \text{ years}$$

$$1980\ T_R = 2.1 \text{ years}$$

$$1986\ T_R = 2.2 \text{ years}$$

It should be pointed out, however, that the estimates of T_R are sensitive to the value of P_A. For example, if P_A were taken to be .85 and not .8, T_R for 1975 would be 3.9 years.

Estimating λ

Estimates of λ were given in Chapter 4 where it was shown that the maximum average values were 5.5, for 1975, 6.4, for 1980 and 10.5, for 1986. Other estimates, derived from samples of offenders, were presented. The average value of λ was about 3, but λ varied between individuals and the 90th percenile was approximately 6.

Estimates of incapacitation effects

Having derived all the parameter estimates Eq 9.1 can be applied to estimate incapacitation effects. In the first analysis incapacitation effects for each of the years 1975, 1980 and 1986 were calculated using the maximum value estimates of λ. Given the uncertainty over the values of T_R, estimates were also derived using Eq 9.2 – Shinnar and Shinnar's simplified model excluding T_R. The results are presented in Table 9.2.

Table 9.2
Estimates of the incapacitation effect of imprisonment; 1975, 1980 and 1986

Year	*Incapacitation effect including T_R*	*Incapacitation effect excluding T_R*
1975	6.2	8.1
1980	5.8	7.2
1986	7.3	9.0

Comparing the two columns in Table 9.2, incorporating an estimate of T_R does not change the inference significantly. Either way levels of imprisonment in the three years did not have a great incapacitation effect. At most imprisonment had the effect of reducing recorded crime by 9.0 per cent from its potential value. And it must be explained that this is the maximum value assuming that all recorded crime is committed by those who are caught. It makes no allowance for co–offending. Further analyses incorporated alternative values of λ, derived from the samples of offenders and presented in Chapter 4, and corrected for co–offending. As expected these analyses (which are not reported here) reduced the estimated incapacitation effects of imprisonment even further.

From the above analyses it can be seen that the current level of imprisonment does not reduce crime by a large amount. This is in accord with the U.S. research. Intuitively the main reason for this is that only a small proportion of offenders are currently given custodial sentences, and many custodial sentences that are given are of a short duration.

Some further, indirect evidence on incapacitation effects is provided by Wolpin (1978)[9.1].

Effects of alternative sentencing policies

The second question posed at the outset of this chapter concerned the effects of general increases or decreases in the use of imprisonment or other custodial sentences on the level of crime. If imprisonment is increased, either by imprisoning more offenders or increasing the time spent in prison by those sentenced to imprisonment (or some combination of the two), the level of crime would be reduced. But by how much? Similarly, less use of imprisonment would be expected to increase crime levels. Obviously if either strategy was adopted it would have implications for the size of the prison population.

There are essentially two ways of estimating the effects of changes in imprisonment. The first is to employ the Shinnar and Shinnar model (Eq 9.1) and change the values of parameters in it, notably S, the proportion of time offenders spend in prison. Of course this model can also be used to assess the effects of other policy options such as changes in J – the probability of being sentenced to imprisonment having been apprehended. A second approach adopted by Petersilia and Greenwood (1978), Van Dine *et. al*. (1977 and 1979) and Brody and Tarling (1980) is simply to take a sample of offenders and simulate what effect an alternative sentence, if it had been imposed in the past, would have had on each offenders' subsequent criminal activity.

Each method is considered and applied.

Modelling changes

The Shinnar and Shinnar model can be adapted to estimate the percentage change in the annual custodial population required to achieve a 1 per cent change in the level of crime. This, the elasticity E, is given by:

$$E = \frac{1 + \lambda qJS^2 T_R \,/\, (T_R + S)^2}{- \lambda qJST_R^2 \,/\, (T_R + S)^2} \qquad \text{Eq. 9.4}$$

[Details of the derivation of this formula are given in Blumstein *et. al.*, 1986, page 146].

By inserting the values for the parameters for each of the three years 1975, 1980 and 1986 in Eq 9.4, E can be estimated. Following this procedure E was found to be:–

1975 E = 18 per cent

1980 E = 20 per cent

1986 E = 16 per cent

Thus in 1975 an 18 per cent increase in the prison population would have been needed to reduce recorded crime by 1 per cent, or, alternatively an 18 per cent reduction in imprisonment would have increased crime by 1 per cent. The corresponding figures for 1980 and 1986 are 20 and 16 per cent. It should be emphasised, moreover, that because the maximum values of λ have been used these are the minimum percentage increases required to reduce crime by 1 per cent. Substituting other, lower, values of λ increased elasticities considerably.

As a comparison the Panel on Criminal Careers estimated elasticities for about 30 U.S. States. E varied between states but was generally in the range 15 to 35.

Simulating changes

A second method is to simulate the effects of changes in the use of imprisonment for a sample of offenders. In the United States this approach has been employed by Petersilia and Greenwood (1978) and Van Dine *et. al.*, (1977 and 1979) and Cohen (1983). Each study took a sample of offenders and calculated, for example, how many offenders in the sample would have been prevented from committing their current offences (that is offences that brought them into the study in the first place), if mandatory prison sentences of varying lengths had been imposed at the time of the previous conviction. The advantage of this method is that it provides a direct measure of incapacitation effects free from making various assumptions about what the offender might have done had he not been in prison. However, the method can only be used to measure the effects of increases in imprisonment. To estimate reductions in imprisonment requires assumptions about what the offender might have done if free in the community.

A similar study was undertaken in this country by Brody and Tarling (1980). Looking at two representative samples of offenders they estimated how many would have been prevented from committing their present offences if an 18 month mandatory prison sentence had been imposed at previous conviction. Given that most prisoners at that time received one third remission of their sentence, an 18 month sentence was equivalent to a net prison sentence of one year (remission has since changed to one half for certain categories of prisoners). Thus all offenders with a previous conviction would have spent one year in prison from the date of that conviction. It is not suggested that this policy be adopted (even if it were not thought too severe, it permits no element of judicial discretion). The analysis was intended simply to give some assessment of the implications of pursuing alternative sentencing policies as a general crime prevention strategy. In addition, changes in the level of imprisonment that would result from such a sentencing policy were estimated by comparing the total length of time the samples of offenders would spend in custody with the total time they actually served.

Since Brody and Tarling's study a third representative sample has become available and results from the analysis of all three are presented here. The first sample included all offenders convicted of an indictable or serious non-indictable offence during March and April 1957 by courts in the Metropolitan Police District. This sample (which will be referred to as the '1957 sample') has been described in more detail in the first and second editions of *The Sentence of the Court* (Home Office, 1964 and 1969). Seventy-six offenders had to be omitted because information necessary for the present analyses was not available. The second sample, the '1971 sample', was a one-in-six random sample of all offenders also convicted of indictable or serious non-indictable offences in January 1971 by all courts in England and Wales (Phillpotts and Lancucki, 1979). The third, the '1987 sample', was a representative sample of offenders sentenced at the Crown Court in 1987 (Moxon, 1988). All three samples originally included female offenders but they have been omitted from this analysis.

The first two samples were approximately equal in size. The 1957 sample comprised 4,163 male offenders who, between them, were convicted of 6,450 offences, and the 1971 sample comprised 4,425 male offenders convicted of 6,714 offences. The 1987 sample comprised 1,851 male offenders convicted of 4,773 offences.

Number of crimes prevented

Of course, first offenders could not have been prevented from committing their sample offences by any sentencing strategy imposed at previous conviction. There were 1,922 first offenders in the 1957 sample and 2,060 in the 1971 sample, representing 46.2 and 46.6 per cent of the totals respectively. The 1987 sample contained proportionally fewer first offenders, 401 or 21.7 per cent – the lower rate being due to the fact that this sample was drawn from those appearing at the Crown Court.

If an 18 month sentence of imprisonment had been imposed at previous conviction on the remainder (2,241 in the 1957 sample, 2,365 in the 1971 sample and 1,450 in the 1987 sample), then only those offenders who had been convicted within the previous year would have been prevented from committing their sample offences. Table 9.3 shows the results of adopting such a strategy.

Table 9.3
Number of offenders and offences prevented by imposing an 18 month mandatory prison sentence at previous conviction

	1957 sample	*1971 sample*	*1987 sample*
Number of offenders	4,163	4,425	1,851
Number of offenders prevented	703	1,095	484
Per cent of offenders prevented	17.4	24.7	26.1
Number of offences	6,475	6,714	4,773
Number of offences prevented	1,200	1,744	1,373
Per cent of offences prevented	18.5	26.0	28.8

It can be seen that the proportion of offenders prevented from committing their sample offences is about the same as the proportion of offences prevented, but both figures have increased somewhat over time. Just over one quarter of the crimes committed by those in the 1987 sample would have been prevented by imposing an 18 month custodial sentence at previous conviction.

Cohen (1983) points out however, that these analyses are retrospective and there is a need for the results to be validated prospectively. (This comment can be applied to all other similar studies.) Prospective validation was possible for the 1971 sample as it is known that about 23 per cent of offenders were reconvicted within one year. Thus if an 18 month sentence had been imposed on all offenders in 1971, 23 per cent would have been prevented from committing further crimes; a result very similar to the proportion (24.7 per cent) who would have been prevented had the sentence been imposed at previous conviction.

The number and type of offences that would have been prevented are shown in Table 9.4

Table 9.4
Number and type of offence prevented by imposing an 18 month prison sentence at previous conviction

Type of offence	*1957 sample*		*1971 sample*		*1987 sample*	
	No.	*Per cent prevented*	*No.*	*Per cent prevented*	*No.*	*Per cent prevented*
Violence against the person	35	25.7	435	23.9	313	20.1
Sexual offences	47	10.6	142	16.2	114	3.2
Burglary and robbery	1,031	25.2	812	51.1	553	33.6
Theft and handling stolen goods	2,708	14.3	2,072	23.6	478	31.5
Fraud and forgery	202	14.4	179	28.5	104	13.5
Malicious or criminal damage	36	25.0	226	23.9	56	25.0
Other (including motoring)	104	24.0	559	13.1	233	19.7
Total	4,163	17.4	4,425	24.7	1,851	26.1

Taking the three samples together, a higher proportion of burglaries and robberies would have been prevented than any other type of offence, while proportionally fewer sexual offences would have been prevented. But imposing incapacitative prison sentences of 18 months would not have prevented any one particular type of crime. Petersilia and Greenwood (1978) and Van Dine *et. al.* (1977) obtained similar results. Thus, there is little evidence that any one type of offence can be prevented by concentrating on those offenders convicted of it on any single occasion. This conclusion is in accord with the results of Chapter 8 where it was shown that offenders specialise in the types of offences they commit only to a limited degree.

Length of time in custody

Had he received an 18 month prison sentence at his last court appearance, each offender with a previous conviction would have spent one year in custody. In the 1957 sample, 2,241 offenders had a previous conviction and so would, between them, have spent 2,241 years in custody for these offences. But in fact only 787 (35.1 per cent) of them were actually given a custodial sentence (imprisonment, approved school, detention centre and borstal) and between them they spent approximately 575 years in custody. (This required making assumptions about the length of time offenders spent in approved schools, detention centres and borstals and assuming that those who qualified for one-third remission of their sentence actually received it.) Therefore, the consequence of adopting such a strategy would have been a nearly four-fold increase in the total length of time this group of offenders spent in custody.

A similar analysis was undertaken for the other two samples. In the 1971 sample 2,365 offenders had a previous conviction and, therefore, would have spent 2,365 years in custody; whereas only 573 (24.2 per cent) of them were actually given a custodial sentence and spent, between them, approximately 325 years in custody[9.2]. Eighteen month mandatory sentences at previous conviction would have resulted in a seven-fold increase in the total length of time this second group of offenders spent in custody. Repeating the analysis for the 1987 sample, 1,450 offenders had a previous conviction and would, therefore, have spent 1,450 years in custody; whereas 444 (30.6 per cent) of them were given a custodial sentence amounting to 218 years in custody[9.3]. Thus a mandatory sentence of 18 months would have increased the time spent in custody by a factor of 6.6.

The estimates provided by the simulation method produce an alternative estimate of the elasticity E, the change in custody needed to achieve a 1 per cent change in the level of crime. For the 1957 sample an approximate 18 per cent reduction in crime would be accomplished by a four-fold increase in custody. Thus to reduce crime by 1 per cent would require a 22 per cent increase in the use of custody. The estimate of E derived from the 1971 sample suggests that a 1 per cent reduction in crime would require a 28 per cent increase in custody. E, derived from the 1987 sample, was found to be 24 per cent. It is interesting to note that these estimates are not too dissimlar to those derived from the model (Eq 9.4) and presented earlier in this chapter bearing in mind that the earlier estimates are minimum values.

A hybrid approach to assessing changes

The previous two sections have considered the effects of alternative sentences by utilising in turn aggregate models and simulation methods. Brody and Tarling (1980) developed an approach which drew from each of these methods. This analysed data on a sample of prisoners and by estimating μ_i for each prisoner assessed the number of additional convictions that would result if prison sentences were reduced. The rate of offending was the subject of Chapter 4. In this application Eq 4.2 was used to calculate μ_i.

Two possible strategies were 'implemented'. The first involved increasing remission from one-third (the level at that time) to one-half. The second reduced the time served by each offender by four months, which, with one-third remission, is equivalent to reducing the sentence awarded by six months. At the time of the study these changes were intended as illustrations although remission has since been increased to one-half for certain categories of prisoners.

Data were available from a one-in-ten random sample of all adult males in prisons in the South East of England in 1972, excluding unconvicted and unsentenced prisoners, civil prisoners and fine defaulters. The overwhelming majority of the men in the sample had been convicted of indictable offences mostly against property; less than 4 per cent had been convicted of non-indictable (mainly motoring) offences. The 40 men in the sample serving life sentences were omitted as the lengths of time they serve and their release are subject to other special considerations which would not be affected by either of the policies evaluated. One other offender also had to be omitted as the necessary information about him was not available. This left a total of 770 prisoners.

By increasing remission from one-third to one-half, each offender in the sample would have spent, on average, 5.7 months less time in prison. From their conviction rates, μ_i, it was estimated that between them they would have accumulated an additional 222 convictions during the extra time they would have been in the community. If the second policy were implemented (reducing the time in prison by four months or reducing the sentence awarded by six months) 64 offenders would not have been sentenced to imprisonment, the remaining 706 would each have spent four months less in prison, and 145 extra convictions could be expected during the additional time they were at liberty.

To assess what effect the two policies would have on the overall number of convictions in any one year, the estimates for the sample had to be extrapolated to the number of offenders leaving prison during the year. To do this the sample had to be reweighted accordingly, because being drawn on a particular day, the sample is only representative of offenders in prison on any one day, not of offenders leaving prison during the year[9.4]. Information on the number of men discharged from prison in 1973 having completed their sentence was provided by the Research and Statistics Department of the Home Office.

The extra number of convictions that could be expected in a year by increasing remission to one-half was found to be approximately 3,500 and the extra number of convictions that could be expected by reducing the time served by four months was found to be approximately 4,500. It may seem surprising that increasing remission would result in fewer extra convictions than reducing the time served by each offender by four months when, for the sample, the opposite result was found. This is a consequence of the reweighting; offenders sentenced to more than two years would spend less time in prison if remission was increased than if they served four months less of their sentence. Conversely, offenders sentenced to less than two years would spend less time in prison if they served four months less of their sentence than if remission was increased. (For offenders sentenced to exactly two years the extra time at liberty would be the same under each policy.) As most offenders sentenced to imprisonment receive fairly short sentences, the total length of time at liberty is greater if each serves four months less than if remission is increased and more convictions would, therefore, be expected.

Approximately 300,000 men were convicted of indictable offences in 1973. Therefore increasing remission to one-half would have increased their convictions by 1.2 per cent and reducing the time served by each offender would have increased convictions by 1.6 per cent.

Length of time in prison[9.5]

Between them the sample of prisoners were serving sentences totalling 2,190 years. If all qualified for one-third remission they would actually spend 1,459 years in prison for their current convictions. Increasing remission to one-half would reduce the time the sample spent in prison by 25 per cent. Reducing the time served by each offender by four months would reduce the time spent in prison by 17 per cent. For all men discharged in 1973, increased remission would reduce the time they spent in prison by 25 per cent and shortening the time served by four months for each offender would reduce the total time spent in prison by 40 per cent[9.6].

Results obtained from this analysis are in accord with those produced by the model and the simulation exercise presented above. A change in the use of custody of the order of 25 per cent would be needed to produce a 1 per cent change in the level of crime.

Selective incapacitation

So far in this chapter it has been shown that the incapacitation effect of current levels of imprisonment is not great. Relatively few crimes would be prevented. A general increase in the use of imprisonment, either by increasing the proportion sentenced to imprisonment, increasing the sentences imposed or increasing the proportion of the sentence that offenders spend in custody, would not affect crime levels by any substantial amount. This would, however, have a significant effect on an already overburdened prison system. One tantalising result from criminal careers research is the considerable variation in the rate at which offenders commit crime; and this was discussed in detail in Chapter 4. It would thus appear on the face of it that if prison sentences were directed specifically at high rate offenders it should be possible to make inroads into the level of crime without necessarily exacerbating the prison system if imprisonment was used more sparingly for other, less frequent, offenders. This then leads to the third question posed at the beginning. Can imprisonment be used in a more specific or selective way to increase its ability to control levels of crime? This issue is usually referred to as selective incapacitation.

The reports emanating from the second RAND inmate survey (Chaiken and Chaiken, 1982, Peterson *et. al.*, 1982, and in particular Greenwood,

1982) provided impetus to the discussion of selective incapacitation in the United States. In the course of this survey about 2,200 jail and prison inmates in three states, California, Michigan and Texas were interviewed and asked to report details of the offences they had committed. Results confirmed the considerable heterogeneity across individuals in their rates of offending. From these data, and other background characteristics supplied by the offenders and obtained from official records, Greenwood identified the factors associated with rates of offending. Seven of the most important were:–

1. Prior conviction for the same offence.
2. Incarcerated more than 50 per cent of preceding two years.
3. Convicted before age 16.
4. Served time in a state juvenile facility.
5. Drug use in preceding 2 years.
6. Drug use as a juvenile.
7. Employed less than 50 per cent of the preceding two years.

These seven factors were used to construct a simple prediction scale: a score of one point being added for each factor if present. Each individual could therefore score between 0 and 7. Individuals scoring 0 or 1 were defined as low rate offenders; a score of 2 or 3 led to a classification as a medium rate offender, 4 or more as a high rate offender. Greenwood then applied this scale to gauge the effects of various hypothetical policy options, such as, increasing the length of time the high rate offenders spend in custody whilst reducing or eliminating the time low and medium rate offenders spend in custody. These options were 'tested' on the different types of offenders in different states.

The most encouraging results were obtained for California. Greenwood estimated that a policy of doubling the sentences for high rate robbery offenders (from about 4 to about 8 years) while limiting sentences for low and medium rate offenders to 'jail' (no more than 1 year) would reduce robbery offences by 20 per cent without increasing the custodial population. For burglary the best policy would reduce burglary by 15 per cent but increase the custodial population by 7 per cent. The results for Texas were less encouraging and more costly in custodial resources; to achieve a 10 per cent reduction in robbery would require a 30 per cent increase in the custodial population and for burglary the same 10 per cent reduction in crime rates would require a 15 per cent increase in custodial resources. The seemingly more successful outcomes in California are simply attributable to the much higher rates of offending reported by Californian inmates. It was not possible for Greenwood to carry out this kind of analysis for Michigan.

Inevitably these claims attracted a good deal of attention and controversy. On the one hand, if true, these claims appear to offer an attractive policy option, a means of reducing crime without incurring an explosion in the prison population, at least in some jurisdictions. On the other hand if these claims are incorrect the consequences of action based upon them are significant. Greenwood's work has, therefore, led to a good deal of debate among the research community including extensive re-analysis of the data. Various criticisms have been raised.

The first set of comments has been directed at the ethical consequences of adopting selective incapacitation policies. Is it right, some have argued, to sentence offenders on the basis of the crimes they might be expected to commit or should offenders only be sentenced for those that they have already committed? Others raise objections to some of the items included in the scale, in particular those beyond the control of the offender – previous employment status is cited an an example. Furthermore, no prediction instrument is correct in every case and some offenders will be misclassified. To be fair, some of these ethical considerations are not specific to Greenwood's work but to the notion of selective incapacitation generally.

Leaving aside ethical objections, the utility of the approach depends on the heterogeneity of offending, the accuracy of the predictions and the ability to discriminate between high, medium and low rate offenders. Greenwood's work has been the subject of considerable methological scrutiny and the Panel commissioned Visher (1986) to reanalyse the RAND data.

Visher carefully reconsidered the way offending rates had been measured and calculated, taking into account other technical issues, such as the problems posed by missing data. Her analysis suggested that estimates of λ for high rate offenders may be too great (although still considerably higher than for low or medium rate offenders). Using her revised calculations Visher reexamined some of the hypothetical policy options presented by Greenwood and found the incapacitation effect to be reduced. For example, she estimated that the reduction in robbery in California would be

13 per cent not 20 per cent as calculated by Greenwood. (Cohen (1983) had also arrived at an estimate of 13 per cent from these data.) Similar policies in Michigan and Texas would probably *increase* crime rates in those states according to Visher. This stems from the fact that the difference in rates of offending between those classified as low, medium and high is not as great as in California and the prediction instrument is not as successful in discriminating between them. Thus in Michigan and Texas the gains in terms of reduction in crime from incarcerating the small number of high rate offenders for longer is more than offset by giving shorter sentences to a large number of low and medium rate offenders who would have more time outside to commit crime (albeit at a lower rate).

To estimate the incapacitation effects of his various policy options, Greenwood used Shinnar and Shinnar's simplified model (Eq 9.2 - discussed previously in this chapter). By not using the full model (Eq 9.1) he made no allowance for career length and the fact that many offenders terminate their careers while in prison. Cohen (1984) assessed the importance of this omission. Applying the same sentencing policy but incorporating estimates of career lengths, she found that crime rates in California would drop by a more modest amount - by about 5 to 10 per cent.

Another methodological problem encountered by prediction studies is that prediction instruments developed on one sample will not perform as well when applied to a different, independent, sample (see Farrington and Tarling 1985, Copas and Tarling, 1986). This phenomenon, usually referred to as *shrinkage*, has been examined in considerable theoretical detail by Copas (1983, 1985). To overcome this problem criminologists have invariably divided their sample randomly into two. One half, 'the construction sample', is used to develop the prediction instrument. The other half, 'the validation sample', is used to assess the degree of shrinkage and to produce an independently validated instrument. Greenwood did not do this or attempt any other validation of his instrument. In the absence of validation it is most likely that his instrument overstates the predictive accuracy that might be achieved.

A final set of comments relates to the practical utility of Greenwood's prediction scale. Various issues are raised if the scale is to be used operationally. The problem of validation and shrinkage has already been mentioned. In addition, Greenwood's scale was developed retrospectively on a sample of inmates. But inmates are unlikely to be representative of all offenders convicted at court yet it is at the sentencing stage that the instrument would be needed. How useful or appropriate would it be at discriminating high rate offenders at conviction is not known. A further point concerns the accuracy of the prediction scale. Following her reanalysis Visher (1986) compared the actual and predicted classification of offenders into low, medium and high rate groups. She found that 46 per cent of the sample were correctly classified by the scale (for example, offenders correctly predicted to be low rate offenders) but 54 per cent were incorrectly classified. This calls into question the utility of the scale to identify high rate offenders in order to give them longer sentences. In particular 55 per cent of those predicted to be high rate offenders were in fact low or medium rate offenders ('false positives').

Perhaps the most telling criticism of the practical benefits of Greenwood's instrument is on a different tack. All but one of the seven items of information (prior conviction for the same offence) used to construct the scale were divulged by the offenders themselves. Hence, in order for this instrument to be of any practical value offenders would be required to admit freely the other six items of information (although some could be obtained from official records, albeit with difficulty, if needed). Offenders are hardly likely to be so forthcoming or truthful if they knew that the information would be used in court to determine their sentence, especially if the sentence was likely to be increased.

Greenwood (1982) himself assessed alternative scales which were actually sub-components of the seven point scale. Greenwood's purpose was to see whether scales excluding items which were likely to raise ethical concerns would be as useful and accurate as the full scale. He constructed two alternative scales (one including the items, prior conviction and incarcerated for more than 50 per cent of preceding two years, the other including these two items plus convicted before age 16 and served time in a state juvenile facility) and found that they performed significantly worse than the original scale. Greenwood went on to estimate the impact these scales would have, if applied, on crime rates and custodial populations. The first sub-scale was found not to be effective for selective incapacitation because it failed to identify a significant number of high rate offenders. The second sub-scale was useable but not useful. For example where the application of the full scale produced a 15 per cent reduction in robbery the sub-scale produced only a 2 per cent reduction. Although Greenwood's primary focus was to exclude items controversial on ethical grounds his analysis did indicate that reduced scales are likely to be of limited use.

Chaiken and Chaiken (1982), in a parallel analysis of the RAND data, directly confronted the issue of restricting the development of prediction instruments to information readily obtainable from official records without relying on self-reported data. Their conclusions are pessimistic; on the whole using official record data "does not provide useful discrimination between high rate and low rate violent predators" (violent predators being a particular sub-group of offenders within the sample) and "no simple, straightforward way of looking at official record data will tell which convicted robbers are the most criminally active." There were several reasons for this. Official records were often lacking or incomplete on key items. In addition criminal records did not always present a similar picture of offending behaviour; for example some juveniles who reported that they committed crimes at a high rate had not been criminally active long enough to amass a long criminal record. In these circumstances prediction instruments based on official records are likely to perform less well.

Because of the ethical issues raised by incorporating particular attributes of offenders and because of the errors of predictions Cohen (1983) considered an alternative approach. She tested various hypothetical sentencing options which entailed giving offenders convicted of certain offences imprisonment of different lengths. A strict 'just deserts' philosophy was pursued; offenders being sentenced for the crimes they had committed with no allowance made for any mitigating, aggravating or background characteristics. Essentially her approach is an extension of that described earlier as simulation methods, the difference being that mandatory sentences varied according to the offence committed rather than being an across the board sentence for all offenders. Leaving to one side whether any form of mandatory sentencing merely raises different ethical issues rather than avoiding them, her results were in line with those suggested by the simulation studies shown in Table 9.5; namely, that more robbery and burglary offences might be prevented by incapacitative sentences but little is to be gained by concentrating on particular types of offence.

A more important finding from her simulations is that shorter prison sentences prevent proportionally more offences than longer sentences. Put another way, the first six months in custody of say, a two year period in custody, will prevent more crimes than the six month period from 18 months to two years. Some prisoners do not reoffend (see Chapter 6), they terminate their careers in prison, so there are likely to be fewer would-be criminals in the second six month period than the first.

10 POLICY IMPLICATIONS AND DIRECTIONS FOR RESEARCH

The fact that many people participate in crime, usually (but not exclusively) during adolescence and that for most offenders involvement in crime is short lived, has led many to advocate minimal intervention by the criminal justice system. It is argued that crime is a passing phase, part of the process of growing up, and most young people should simply be allowed to grow out of crime (see, for example, Rutherford, 1986). The natural processes of maturation are sufficient and should be allowed to take their course. Stigmatising or labelling by the criminal justice system may only make matters worse. Such a policy has been broadly accepted and adopted in this country and many Western European countries for most juvenile offenders (those under 17 years of age). Here, the use of police cautioning has continued to grow while the imposition of custodial sentences for juveniles has fallen substantially.

More recent policy debate has focussed on persistent juvenile and young adult offenders who do not terminate their careers early. These are often offenders who began their careers at an early age and have developed extensive criminal records by their mid to late teens and early twenties. Of course, not all adult offenders are persistent offenders. A significant proportion of offenders do not begin their careers until adulthood and, like many juveniles, their involvement in crime is short lived. But it is often amongst the ranks of young adult offenders that more persistent offenders are to be found. Looked at another way, all cohort studies have found that a small proportion of the cohort accounts for a significant proportion of the crimes committed by the cohort. This finding has had an important impact on policy thinking, for if the small group of persistent offenders could be identified, a successful policy devised and implemented to reduce their offending would lead to significant reductions in crime. In the U.S. this has led to calls to increase the use of imprisonment to incapacitate offenders, a policy much criticised by Gottfredson and Hirschi (1990). However, interest there in incapacitation seems to be waning following research evidence pointing out the limitations of such a policy.

Increasing the general use of imprisonment to counter crime does not appear to be a cost effective option. It was pointed out in Chapter 9 that to reduce recorded crime in this country by 1 per cent might require a 25 per cent increase in the prison population. Selective incapacitation, reserving custody for persistent offenders while reducing it for less persistent ones (which would bring the benefits of reductions in crime without increasing prison populations), is not without problems. To have any significant impact, high rate or persistent offenders have to be identified at the start of, or at an early stage in, their careers. All attempts to do this have been unsuccessful, at least with a degree of accuracy that would be acceptable in order to pursue such a policy. Leaving aside the ethical issue of sentencing people for crimes they have not yet committed, all prediction instruments so far devised would result in too many 'false positives', offenders predicted to be persistent offenders who in fact were not. The best predictor of future offending is past offending but if one has to wait until persistent offenders identify themselves by amassing an extensive criminal career much of the potential of selective incapacitation is lost.

The realisation that imprisonment is not only costly but is of limited value both in preventing crime and in rehabilitating offenders, has resulted in policy shifting towards the greater use of community penalties, at least for property offenders. Punishment should be commensurate with the seriousness of the offence and for most property offenders this can be achieved by punishment in the community, "with greater emphasis on bringing home to the criminal the consequences of his actions, compensation to the victims and reparation to the community". Furthermore, "the prospects of reforming offenders are usually much better if they stay in the community" (Home Office, 1990). Imprisonment is seen increasingly as a sanction to be used for those serious offenders who pose a threat to public safety.

Research on offending has influenced policy thinking in other directions. The factors associated with offending, reviewed in Chapter 5, stress the importance of early life experiences such as the quality of family upbringing, school achievement and aspects of social disadvantage as well as factors such as drug and alcohol dependency. These factors often pre-date any formal contact with, or are outside the ambit of, the criminal justice system. Farrington (1989b), summarising the lessons to be learned from the Cambridge Study of Delinquent Development, believes that addressing these wider social problems is likely to be the most effective way of preventing offending. Gottfredson and Hirschi agree; for them low self control leads to criminal behaviour and the origins of self control are to be found in early childhood socialisation – during the first six to eight years of life. For Farrington and Gottfredson and Hirschi the emphasis is on the early prevention of crime rather than the treatment or rehabilitation of known offenders by the criminal justice system.

Following earlier enthusiasm, reviews of the research evidence (Martinson, 1974, Brody, 1976) led to the demise of rehabilitation as an objective of the criminal justice system. This is now being reassessed. The U.S. National Academy of Sciences Panel on Rehabilitation of Offenders reassessed the research evidence and decided that rehabilitation as such had not been discredited. The Panel concluded that rehabilitation had not proved successful to date simply because many programmes had not been properly implemented. In addition, the Panel claimed that the actual evaluation of many programmes had been so inadequate that any genuine positive benefits had not been identified. (Sechrest *et. al.*, 1979 and Martin *et. al.*, 1981).

In the past too much was expected of the criminal justice system and inevitably it failed to live up to those expectations. Now there is more realism; it is generally accepted that the criminal justice system can play only a limited part in reforming offenders. A probation officer may be able to help a probationer with current debt management problems but he or she cannot provide for the offender a life of financial solvency. A few hours per week of education during a short custodial sentence cannot rectify a decade of educational under-achievement. And a short drug abuse treatment programme provided by a criminal justice system agency cannot be expected to break the habits of a lifetime.

Future policy developments have been advocated which place greater emphasis on social or community crime prevention strategies. Examples are training parents in effective child rearing methods, pre-school intellectual enrichment programmes, and other ways of compensating for social adversity and of addressing the problems of crime-prone environments and communities (Eisenhower Foundation, 1990, Hope and Shaw, 1988 and Wilson and Herrnstein, 1985). The implementation of such policies will require the involvement of agencies outside the formal criminal justice system. As to future criminal justice system programmes, they need to be more focussed, helping to tackle offenders' specific problems in order to assist their reintegration into communities. Many probation services are developing specific programmes for drug, sexual and motoring offenders as well as addressing offenders' cognitive skills. But the programmes should have clear and realistic objectives, be properly implemented and judged against those objectives.

Directions for further research

Criminal career research has sparked off a dispute about research agendas and the appropriate methodological approaches required to study offending. Blumstein *et. al.*, 1986, and Farrington *et. al.*, 1986, amongst others have advocated more longitudinal or cohort studies to examine career progression and the crucial life events bearing upon it. Such studies would clarify further the causal factors leading to criminal behaviour.

Gottfredson and Hirschi (1990) are forceful critics of the supposed need for additional longitudinal studies. They argue that the disproportionate cost of this research design is not likely to represent value for money. Most of the facts that have been identified by longitudinal studies have been revealed by simple cross-sectional studies. Furthermore, it is not necessary to follow cohorts prospectively to measure life events such as going to school or getting married, since this information can be gathered retrospectively. They question the superiority of longitudinal design in clarifying causality: "we can observe offenders every hour of the day and still not know the causes of their behaviour".

There are merits in both points of view but unfortunately the debate has become unnecessarily polarised. Cross-sectional studies and longitudinal studies are ideal types, and in reality research designs are often somewhere in between. A cross-sectional design, which draws a sample at one point in time, invariably has elements of a longitudinal study. Information on the subjects' past can be assembled retrospectively and subjects are sometimes followed up prospectively for a limited period of time. Longitudinal studies need not always be prospective. Cohorts and longitudinal data can sometimes be constructed retrospectively from existing information systems if the appropriate data are recorded. The Research and Statistics Department cohorts (discussed in earlier chapters) were assembled in this way. Cost considerations are not always in favour of cross-sectional designs. The Research and Statistics Department cohorts were relatively cheap to construct and it may often cost less to follow up existing cohorts, where the subjects are already selected and much of the information assembled, than start from the beginning with a new cross-sectional study.

If it is true, as Gottfredson and Hirschi claim, that the same inferences result from cross-sectional studies and longitudinal studies, then that itself has proved a sufficient justification for adopting both approaches in the past (although it might also support their argument of a limited role for longitudinal studies in the future). Generally, greater confidence can be placed in findings if they stem from a variety of methodologies. There can be no absolutes in research design; it was pointed out in Chapter 1 that the topic to be examined will govern the way to proceed. There is a place for all approaches.

Existing cohorts should be followed up in order to provide more accurate information about some of the key parameters of criminal careers. Estimates of the length of criminal careers, discussed in Chapter 4, were derived from cohorts followed up until their early thirties so it is not known how long those still active in their early thirties continued their career and at what point they stopped committing crime. Furthermore, it is not known how many of those who appear to cease their careers in adolescence return to crime in later life. Following up existing cohorts could give information on rates of offending by age for older age groups, as well as further estimates of participation in offending. At present, life table methods provide some measure of participation for older age groups.

Successive cohorts are needed to assess the extent to which the basic parameters change between different generations. In Britain, however, this poses problems. It was pointed out in Chapter 3 that many offenders are now dealt with by means of a police caution. Information on convictions at court is no longer sufficient to measure accurately patterns of known offending for later generations. Information on police cautions needs to be added. Unfortunately, details of police cautions cannot be linked easily to court convictions and collating cautions and convictions will require considerable effort.

Research will continue to be directed at distinguishing the persistent, repeat or frequent offenders from those offenders who commit just one or two offences and then terminate their careers; or put another way, distinguishing factors contributing to *participation* from those contributing to *frequency* of offending. While the research should continue it may prove difficult to identify in advance future persistent offenders. Research to date indicates that the same factors are related to participation as to frequency. Furthermore, Blumstein and Moitra (1980) have pointed out that even if all offenders have the same propensity to commit crime, in any sample chance alone would result in some offenders committing many more crimes than other offenders (this was discussed in Chapter 4). Identifying frequent offenders is a complex methodological task and the statistical problems posed have been emphasised recently by Nagin and Smith (1990). They also propose a series of tests to handle the intricate problems. More work is called for on this theoretical issue together with applications to criminal career data.

If offenders do not persist in offending they desist or terminate their careers. But little specific research has been carried out on why offenders stop offending or on what influences that decision. (The research to date is summarised in Chapter 5.) Desistance could be a profitable area for future research with important policy implications.

In addition to age, gender is the major correlate of crime. Yet while the criminal career debate has prompted research and discussion of age and crime it has not led to a similar interest concerning the differences in rates of offending between males and females. Increasingly, female crime is receiving attention from feminist writers but it appears that this is being conducted outside the mainstream of criminal career research. Research on female crime is limited in comparison with the amount of research on male offending.

In this study, parallel analyses of female offenders were undertaken wherever possible and it is hoped that this will contribute to greater understanding of the relationship between age, sex and type of offence committed, the length of criminal careers, co-offending and reoffending. Surprisingly, perhaps, many similarities were found between female and male offenders. But the results do not explain why fewer females than males commit crime. What is it about the individual motivation of females, their socialisation, lifestyles, experiences and social mores which inhibits them from committing crime? More comparative research of male and female offenders and non-offenders may illuminate the importance of gender as a correlate of crime.

In this country, more research may be needed on the relationship between race and crime, if only to provide a means of addressing the concern that has been expressed about possible racial discrimination by the criminal justice system. It was pointed out in Chapter 5 that only one cohort study and no self-report studies conducted in this country included any members from ethnic minorities and few subsequent studies have examined the differential involvement in crime by different groups. Any further studies should examine the types of crime committed by different ethnic groups, and it will be necessary to control for other known correlates of crime in order that any findings of differential involvement in crime can be placed in context.

Insufficient detailed evidence is available about how community characteristics relate to the development or to the termination of criminal careers. This issue is likely to assume greater significance if the thrust of policy is to place greater emphasis on dealing with offenders in the community. Notwithstanding the considerable research that has been undertaken on gangs of juveniles, further research may be needed on the effects of communities on crime. This should include how older offenders become attached to social networks and subcultures, the type and depth of that involvement and the mechanisms for successfully reintegrating offenders in the community.

Despite the disagreement on some aspects of research design there is consensus on the need for greater experimentation. Properly conducted, controlled experiments, preferably involving randomisation, are especially valuable in evaluating policy initiatives and programmes of the kind discussed in the previous section. In addition to controlled experiments, researchers should be more alert to capitalise on the many opportunities provided in the criminal justice area which allow 'natural experiments'. For example, different approaches are adopted in various parts of the country and this can provide a 'natural' opportunity to evaluate variations in the practical implementation of broad policies.

Nevertheless, whatever the prospects of conducting more experiments, a significant proportion of research and evaluation will need to call upon statistical methods to disentangle causal relationships and the effects of alternative programmes and policies. Higher standards of evaluation will be required. The findings presented earlier have a bearing on this methodological issue; for example, when investigating subsequent offending, research emphasises the need to control for previous offending in particular and also the age of the offender. The 'continuance probabilities' (presented in Chapter 4) reinforce the importance of previous offending. It was shown there that about one third of males received one conviction. Of those males getting one conviction, about one half to two-thirds will be convicted again, and of those with two convictions between two-thirds and three-quarters will be convicted a third time, and so on. Thus, previous offending must be controlled for in any evaluation. The success of a programme or sentence must be judged against what would generally be expected for that group of offenders. No meaningful comparison of alternative programmes or sentences is possible unless the type of offenders given those sentences is properly taken into account. Furthermore, if the type of offenders given a sentence changes due to a change in sentencing policy, or the programme is targetted at different types of offender, then the rates and patterns of subsequent offending will also change, irrespective of the success of the sentence or programme in rehabilitating offenders. This is an obvious point but one that is often overlooked.

The development of appropriate statistical models will have an important part to play in understanding offending and in evaluating policy interventions. Survival models, discussed in Chapter 6, address the time to the next event (in this case the time to the next offence) and introduce the important concept of the hazard rate, that is, the probability that an offender will offend at some point in time if he has not reoffended up to that point.

Survival models are routinely used in medical and industrial research and their application in criminology is growing. They are superior to traditional methods of analysing recidivism data. Standard survival models assume that every subject will fail eventually and do not allow for the fact that some offenders will not reoffend because they terminate their careers. Criminologists have thus extended survival models and developed split population models which take account of career termination. Such models have great theoretical appeal and may be useful in analysing and understanding persistence and desistance referred to earlier. However, the problems experienced by those who have attempted to develop split population models incorporating covariates indicate that this will not be straightforward.

Survival models are appropriate when the focus of interest is the time from some point in a career (for example, when an offender is released from prison) to the next offence. More generally, however, criminal careers are made up of several offences committed over a period of time. Stochastic models are necessary to understand the timing of successive offences. They have not received as much attention from criminologists as survival models but the work to date was summarised in Chapter 7. Stochastic models of criminal careers have been conceptualised in different ways; some have extended models to accommodate changes in the rate of offending and the influence of different background factors while others have developed the notion of split population models to incorporate career termination.

Criminal careers can be conceptualised in another way; as being of a certain duration with offenders differing in the length of time that they are criminally active. Such a model was developed in Chapter 7. Work on stochastic models is at an early stage of development and once cohorts have been followed up for a further period of time and the data base extended, they could be re-examined. For example, it will be possible to reconsider the model of career length when more accurate information on desistance is available. Furthermore, models which have assumed the rate of offending to be constant throughout an active offender's criminal career will need to be modified if it is found that the rate declines for older age groups. There is evidence to suggest that this is the case.

Survival models and stochastic models, which adequately represent the underlying processes, will also be needed to evaluate programmes and policies. This is particularly true where the nature of any relationship is complex or subtle differences in effects are to be detected. Moreover, if the effects of the criminal justice system are limited, as stated above, then more sensitive methods will be needed to identify them. Models which address the time to the next offence or the time interval between offences will be particularly important in evaluating programmes which may vary in duration between offenders. An example here is the recent change in sentencing policy which will entail offenders spending some time in prison and some time being supervised in the community. The length of time of community supervision will vary according to the sentence imposed.

On a more immediate and practical level, models are being developed to aid management decisions. Parole authorities have used risk prediction scores for a long time to help determine whether and when prisoners should be released on parole. Similar aids to decision-making are being developed which will target the kinds of offenders most suitable for other forms of intervention and selection for particular programmes.

This report has summarised the substantial body of reseach into the incidence of offending and criminal careers. But our understanding of offending is far from complete. Offending is a complex phenomenon, stemming from the interplay of personal, social and cultural characteristics. There are no simple solutions or policy prescriptions. The agenda for research, outlined above, is not exhaustive. But more research is needed, coupled with more creative thinking and experimental and developmental programmes to identify effective approaches and to guide future policy innovations.

Notes

1.1 In England and Wales the police have the power to caution an offender who admits an offence rather than initiate court proceedings. Police cautions, which take the form of an official reprimand from the police, are given, in the main, to juveniles and elderly offenders who have committed a less serious offence and who do not have an extensive criminal record.

1.2 In addition to the number of persons found guilty or cautioned in each year there are a small number of other offenders (companies etc.). In 1988, for example, there were about 2,700 such offenders. Where possible these have been omitted from the data presented in this report.

2.1 It should be remembered that a person may be dealt with on more than one occasion in any one year. To this extent yearly aggregate statistics will be a combination of the number of people who participate in crime and incidence, the rate at which people commit crime in one year. However, as most people are only dealt with once in a year, the aggregate statistics closely reflect participation rates.

2.2 For some offences not considered here, in particular 'white collar crimes', the peak age of offending may be much higher. Some supportive evidence is provided in the section **Self-reported offending** in Chapter 3. Offences such as; stealing office supplies or pilfering from work, fiddling work expenses, tax evasion or evading customs duties were more likely to be committed by people aged 22 to 40 than by younger people.

3.1 Mitchell and Rosa (1981) also present data on convictions obtained by a sub-set of a cohort in Buckinghamshire. However, the sub-set was selected in such a way as to make estimates of participation for the cohort as a whole problematic.

3.2 Little (1965) undertook a similar study to McClintock and Avison based on 1962 data. However, as he only presented estimates up to the age of 21 his results are not given prominence here. In fact the results are, as one might expect, slightly lower than the 1965 estimates: 16 per cent of males and 2.6 of females were convicted by age 21. Little also presented data on arrests for indictable offences in the Metropolitan Police District for persons born in 1942. He did this by adding up first arrests for 8 year olds in 1950, 9 year olds in 1951 etc. Unfortunately the data he used did not separate males from females so it is impossible to draw any comparisons with other data. Little's main aim was not to derive detailed estimates but to discuss the differences between the two methodologies: cohort or longitudinal follow–up studies and the life table approach.

3.3 The key assumptions in this analysis are the proportion of those convicted who had been previously cautioned and the extent to which more than one caution is given to any one person. It would seem from the cautioning research, that the assumption that most convicted males had previously been cautioned may not be far out although rather more females receive multiple cautions, as cautioning is a more frequent method of dealing with female offenders. Further confirmation of these results can be obtained if data for males and females are combined and compared with the Greater Manchester Police data (which are combined). From the cohort studies 12.2 per cent of males and 2.3 per cent of females were convicted as juveniles, overall 7.3 per cent were convicted. 67,700 males and 21,600 females born in 1963 were cautioned as juveniles. Thus the participation rate including cautions was 11.1 per cent or 52 per cent higher than for convictions alone. This is very similar to the 47 per cent increase found from the Greater Manchester Police data.

3.4 As many arrests do not result in court appearance and conviction and as court records are generally more difficult to obtain, most U.S. studies of offending examine police records for information on arrests. As an indication of how participation rates can be inflated, if status offences and liquor violations are included the participation rate for the first Philadelphia birth cohort rises to 34.9 per cent. A subset of 975 members of the cohort was followed up to age 30 by which time 47.1 per cent had been arrested for a non traffic offence (Wolfgang et. al., 1987).

3.5 This figure is taken from Farrington (1986) who obtained it from personal communication with Wolf. The figure in Wolf (1984) is 35 per cent but this includes many minor motoring offences.

4.1 It is not appropriate to apply this form of analysis to cross–sectional samples of offenders, such as the sample of those appearing at the

Crown Court or the sample of parolees, as offenders within each are of different ages and at different points in their careers.

4.2 It is of interest to note that had court appearances been used instead of convictions a broadly similar pattern emerges but the probabilities are slightly lower at each stage in the sequence. Thus for males the corresponding figures are: 1 = .33, 2 = .45, 3 = .64, 4 = .72, 5 = .77, 6 = .77, 7 = .78 and 8 onwards about .81. For females the figures are: 1 = .07, 2 = .23, 3 = .46, 4 = .59, 5 = .58, 6 = .74, 7 = .69 and 8 onwards about .82.

4.3 Blumstein and Moitra (1980) denoted the final probability by q. Here r is used to avoid confusion with q which is used in this report to denote the probability of being cautioned or convicted following the commission of a crime.

4.4 The rate of convictions μ in Table 4.6 differs somewhat from those shown in Table 4.5. Not too much should be made of this; estimates in Table 4.5 were for more active offenders whereas the analysis presented in Table 4.6 included all offenders. Furthermore, it was assumed in the analysis for Table 4.6 that an offender who had at least one conviction within any time period was active during the whole of that period. This assumption is not strictly correct as some offenders will have terminated their career before the end of the period. The longer the period the more likely offenders will terminate their career and the rates for age group 25 < 31 may, in part, be low for that reason.

6.1 The maximum likelihood estimator of θ is equal to $n/\Sigma t_i$, where n is the number who reoffend and t_i is the time to reoffend (for those who reoffend) or the time to the end of the follow up period (censoring point) for those who do not reoffend.

6.2 To avoid confusion with λ, the rate of offending, λ in Aitken et. al. (1989) has been replaced by γ. The GLIM parameterisation is slightly different to that of Schmidt and Witte, 1988, p57. γ in Aitken et. al. is equivalent to θ^k in Schmidt and Witte.

6.3 The split exponential and the split Weibull were developed using GAUSS, a matrix language computer package.

6.4 Cox's proportional hazards model was fitted using the statistical package BMDP. Jagger and Clayton (1981) show how this model can be fitted by GLIM.

7.1 A number of more complicated non-markovian models that could allow for such a correlation have been developed in the stochastic process literature, but their usefulness in criminological research remains unexplored.

7.2 In fact Dugdale (1989) only analysed data for a sample of the cohort. He randomly selected one day of the four week period, his sample being all those born on that day. Thus his sample comprised about 4 per cent of the original cohort.

7.3 This was due to the fact that Dugdale analysed data for only a subset of the data (see note 7.2).

7.4 Dugdale's (1989) results are not directly comparable with results presented in chapter 4 of this report. μ_i in his study relates to court appearances whereas the results in Table 4.5 are for convictions. Furthermore, only joint estimates for males and females together are given and only a subset of the cohort was analysed (see Note 7.2).

7.5 I am extremely grateful to Professor John B Copas, Department of Statistics, Birmingham University, for his advice and assistance in developing this model.

8.1 Although the first offence was committed as a juvenile, for some the second, reconviction, offence may have been commited after age 16, that is as an adult.

8.2 When ASRs were calculated on the complete matrices many of the off-diagonal elements were found to be lower than expected. None were found to be higher than expected.

8.3 The analysis was carried out using the GLIM statistical package by 'weighting out' the main diagonals. An alternative procedure is to include the main diagonal elements and to fit a log-linear model constraining the fitted main diagonal elements to their observed values. This model is often referred to as the 'mover-stayer' model (from social mobility) and is described by Fingleton (1984). It is similar to the 'main diagonal' model except that the variable representing the main diagonal elements is not dichotomous (merely representing whether or not the element is on the main diagonal) but has a separate parameter for each of the main diagonal elements (in this case 10 or 5). The mover-stayer model and the model eliminating the main diagonal are in fact equivalent and produced the same results.

9.1 Wolpin (1978) analysed time series data for England and Wales for the years 1894 to 1967 excluding the years 1914–19 and 1939–45. Wolpin included a measure of the average length of prison sentences imposed in each of the years, but did not find this to be significantly related to the crime rate, a result which implies only a small incapacitation effect, if any. However, as he pointed out, average length of sentence is not a very appropriate index, and if it had been possible instead to include average length of time served, a stronger relationship might have emerged.

9.2 Estimates of the total time in prison are likely to be overestimates as some prisoners will have been released earlier on parole licence. The increase in the time spent in prison following mandatory sentences is therefore likely to be underestimated. (Parole was not in operation in 1957).

9.3 See note 9.2 above.

9.4 Compared with the number of offenders leaving prison in any one year, the sample inevitably over-represented offenders given long sentences (as their chances of being in prison on the day the sample is drawn is greater) and under-represented those given short sentences. For example, approximately 60 per cent of offenders discharged from prison during 1973 had completed sentences of less than 12 months, whereas only a quarter of the prison sample was serving sentences of a similar length. In order to estimate increases in the number of convictions for the year, the sample was divided into sub-groups according to the length of sentence being served. Conviction rates were calculated within each sub-group and then multiplied by the number of offenders discharged during 1973 after completing similar sentences.

9.5 These estimates do not take into account the fact that some prisoners were released early on parole licence. It is assumed that time on parole remains constant. However, reducing sentence length would reduce the number of prisoners eligible for parole or make them eligible for a shorter proportion of their sentence. To this extent the figures are in error.

9.6 Individual sentence lengths are not given, only the number of offenders within sentence bands (eg not more than one month, over one and up to 3 months, etc). The estimates given are, therefore, approximations.

References

Aitkin, M. and Francis, B. (1980). 'A GLIM macro for fitting the exponential or Weibull distribution to censored data'. *GLIM Newsletter*, June, 19–25.

Aitkin, M., Anderson, D., Francis, B. and Hinde, J. (1989). *Statistical Modelling in GLIM*. Oxford: Oxford University Press.

Allison, P. D. (1984). *Event History Analysis*. Quantitative Applications in the Social Sciences, 46, Beverly Hills: Sage Publications.

Avi-Itzhak, B. and Shinnar, R. (1973). 'Quantitative models in crime control'. *Journal of Criminal Justice*, 1, 185–217.

Barnett, A., Blumstein, A. and Farrington, D. P. (1987). 'Probabilistic models of youthful criminal careers'. *Criminology*, 25, 83–107.

Barnett, A., Blumstein, A. and Farrington, D. P. (1989). 'A prospective test of a criminal career model'. *Criminology*, 27, 373–388.

Barton, R. R. and Turnbull, B. W. (1979). 'Failure rate regression models for evaluation of recidivism data'. *Evaluation Quarterly*, 3, 629–41.

Barton, R. R. and Turnbull, B. W. (1981). 'A failure rate regression model for the study of recidivism'. In: J. A. Fox (Ed.). *Models in Quantitative Criminology*. New York: Academic Press.

Bean, P. and Wilkinson, C. (1988). 'Drug taking, crime and the illicit supply system'. *British Journal of Addiction*, 83, 533–39.

Belson, W. A. (1975). *Juvenile Theft: The Causal Factors*. London: Harper and Row.

Bennett, T. and Wright, R. (1984). 'The relationship between alcohol use and burglary'. *British Journal of Addiction*, 79, 431–38.

Blumstein, A and Cohen, J. (1979). Estimation of individual crime rates from arrest records'. *Journal of Criminal Law and Criminology*, 70, 561–585.

Blumstein, A., Cohen, J., Das, S. and Moitra, S. D. (1988). 'Specialization and seriousness during adult criminal careers'. *Journal of Quantitative Criminology*, 4, 303–345.

Blumstein, A., Cohen, J. and Farrington, D. P. (1988). 'Criminal career research: its value for criminology'. *Criminology*, 26, 1–35.

Blumstein, A., Cohen, J. and Nagin, D. (Eds.). (1978). *Deterrence and Incapacitation*. Washington, D.C.: National Academy of Sciences.

Blumstein, A., Cohen, J., Roth, J. A. and Visher, C. A. (1986). *Criminal Careers and "Career Criminals"*. Vols I and II. Washington, D.C.: National Academy of Sciences.

Blumstein, A., Farrington, D. P. and Moitra, S. (1985). 'Delinquency careers: innocents, desisters and persisters'. In: Tonry, M. and Morris, N. (Eds.). *Crime and Justice: An Annual Review of Research*, Vol 6. Chicago: University of Chicago Press.

Blumstein, A. and Moitra, S. (1980). 'The identification of 'Career Criminals' from 'Chronic Offenders in a cohort.' *Law and Policy Quarterly*, 2, 321–24.

Bottoms, A. E. (1967). 'Delinquency among immigrants'. *Race*, 8, 4.

Bottoms, A. E. (1973). 'Crime and delinquency in immigrant and minority groups'. In: Watson, P. (Ed.). *Psychology and Race*. Harmondsworth: Penguin.

Box, S. (1971). *Deviance, Reality and Society*. London: Holt, Rinehart & Winston.

Brody, S. R. (1976). *The Effectiveness of Sentencing*. Home Office Research Study No. 35. London: HMSO.

Brody, S. R. and Tarling, R. (1980). *Taking Offenders out of Circulation*. Home Office Research Study No.64. London: HMSO

Burrows, J. and Tarling, R. (1982). *Clearing up Crime*. Home Office Research Study No. 73. London: HMSO.

Burrows, J. and Tarling, R. (1987). 'The investigation of crime in England and Wales'. *British Journal of Criminology*, 27, 229–51.

Bursik, R. J. (1980). 'The dynamics of specialization in juvenile offences'. *Social Forces*, 58, 851–864.

Carr-Hill, G. A. and Carr-Hill, R. A. (1972). 'Reconviction as a process'. *British Journal of Criminology*, 12, 35–43.

Carr-Hill, R. A. and Payne, C. D. (1971). 'Crime: accident or disease: an exploration using probability models for the generation of macro-criminological data'. *Journal of Research in Crime and Delinquency*, 8, 133–155.

Chaiken, J. M. and Chaiken, M. (1982). *Varieties of Criminal Behavior*. Santa Monica, Calif.: Rand Corporation.

Clarke, S. H. (1975). 'Getting 'em out of circulation: does incarceration of juvenile offenders reduce crime?' *Journal of Criminal Law and Criminology*, 65, 528–35.

Cohen, J. (1978). 'The incapacitative effect of imprisonment: a critical review of the literature'. In: A. Blumstein, J. Cohen and D. Nagin (Eds.). *Deterrence and Incapacitation: Estimating the Effects of Criminal*

Sanctions on Crime Rates. Washington D.C.: National Academy of Sciences.

COHEN, J. (1983). 'Incapacitation as a strategy for crime control: possibilities and pitfalls'. In: M. Tonry and N. Morris (Eds.). *Crime and Justice an Annual Review of Research, Volume 5*. Chicago: University of Chicago Press.

COHEN, J. (1984). 'Selective incapacitation: An assessment'. *University of Illinois Law Review*, 253–90.

COHEN, J. (1986). 'Research on criminal careers: Individual frequency rates and offense seriousness'. In: A. Blumstein, J. Cohen, J. Roth and C. A. Visher. (Eds.). *Criminal Careers and "Career Criminals", Vol I*. Washington D.C.: National Academy Press.

COPAS, J. B. (1983). 'Regression, prediction and shrinkage'. *Journal of the Royal Statistical Society, Series B*, 45, 311–54.

COPAS, J. B. (1985). 'Prediction equations, statistical analysis and shrinkage'. In: D. Farrington and R. Tarling. (Eds.). *Prediction in Criminology*. Albany, New York: SUNY.

COPAS, J. B. AND TARLING, R. (1986). 'Some methodological issues in making predictions'. In: A. Blumstein, J. Cohen, J. A. Roth and C. A. Visher (Eds.). *Criminal Careers and "Career Criminals"*. Vol II. Washington, D.C.: National Academy of Sciences.

COPAS, J. B. AND TARLING, R. (1988). 'Stochastic models for analyzing criminal careers'. *Journal of Quantitative Criminology*, 4, 173–86.

COX, D. R. (1972). 'Regression models and life tables'. *Journal of the Royal Statistical Society, Series B*, 34, 187–220.

COX, D. R. (1975). 'Partial likelihood'. *Biometrika*, 62, 276–96.

COX, D. R. AND OAKES, D. (1984). *Analysis of Survival Data*. London: Chapman and Hall.

DITCHFIELD, J. (1989). 'Offending on parole'. *Research Bulletin* No. 26, 13–16. London: Home Office Research and Planning Unit.

DONNELL, A. A. AND LOVELL, R. J. (1982). *How Many Offend*. Wellington, New Zealand: Young Offenders Research Unit, Department of Social Welfare.

DOUGLAS, J., ROSS, J. AND SIMPSON, H. (1968). *All Our Future*. London: Peter Davies.

DUGDALE, S. J. (1989). *Stochastic Compartmental Models for Analysing Criminal Careers*. Phd Thesis, School of Mathematics and Statistics, University of Birmingham.

EASTERLIN, R. A. (1980). *Birth and Fortune*. New York: Basic Books.

The Milton S. Eisenhower Foundation. (1990). *Youth Investment and Community Reconstruction*. Washington D.C.: The Milton S Eisenhower Foundation.

Farrington, D. P. (1981). 'The prevalence of convictions'. *British Journal of Criminology*, 2, 173–5.

Farrington, D. P. (1983). *Further Analysis of a Longitudinal Survey of Crime and Delinquency*. Washington D.C.: National Institute of Justice.

Farrington, D. P. (1986). 'Age and crime'. In: M. Tonry and N. Morris (Eds.). *Crime and Justice, Volume 7*. Chicago: University of Chicago Press.

Farrington, D. P. (1989a). 'Self-reported and official offending from adolescence to adulthood'. In: M. W. Klein (Ed.). *Cross-National Research in Self-Reported Crime and Delinquency*. Dordrecht, The Netherlands: Kluwer Academic Publishers.

Farrington, D. P. (1989b). 'The origins of crime: the Cambridge Study in Delinquent Development'. *Research Bulletin* No. 27, 29–32. London: Home Office Research and Planning Unit.

Farrington, D. P., Ohlin, L. E. and Wilson, J. Q. (1986). *Understanding and Controlling Crime*. New York: Springer-Verlag.

Farrington, D. P., Snyder, H. N. and Finnegan, T. A. (1988). 'Specialization in juvenile court careers'. *Criminology*, 26, 461–487.

Farrington, D. P. and Tarling, R. (1985). *Prediction in Criminology*. Albany, New York: SUNY.

Fingleton, B. (1984). *Models of Category Counts*. Cambridge: Cambridge University Press.

Gladstone, F. J. (1978). 'Vandalism amongst adolescent schoolboys'. In: Clarke, R. V. G. (Ed.). *Tackling Vandalism*. Home Office Research Study No. 47. London: HMSO.

Goodman, L. A. (1962). 'Statistical methods for analyzing processes of change'. *American Journal of Sociology*, 68, 461–487.

Gottfredson, M. (1984). *Victims of Crime: The Dimension of Risk*. Home Office Research Study No. 81. London: HMSO.

Gottfredson, M. and Hirschi, T. (1986). 'The true value of lamda would appear to be zero'. *Criminology*, 24, 213–34.

Gottfredson, M. and Hirschi, T. (1987). 'The methodological adequacy of longitudinal research on crime'. *Criminology*, 25, 581–614.

Gottfredson, M. and Hirschi, T. (1988). 'Science, public policy, and the career paradigm'. *Criminology*, 26, 37–55.

Gottfredson, M. and Hirschi, T. (1990). *A General Theory of Crime*. Stanford California: Stanford University Press.

Greenberg, D. F. (1975). 'The incapacitative effect of imprisonment: some estimates.' *Law and Society Review*, 9, 541–80.

Greenwood, P. (1982). *Selective Incapacitation*. Santa Monica, Calif.: Rand Corporation.

Haberman, S. J. (1979). *Analysis of Qualitative Data, Vol 2*. New York: Academic Press.

Hammersley, R., Morrison, V., Davies, J. B. and Forsyth, A. (1990). *Heroin Use and Crime*. Central Research Unit Papers. Edinburgh: Scottish Office.

Harris, C. M., Kaylan, A. R. and Maltz, M. D. (1981). 'Refinements in the statistics of recidivism measurement'. In: J. A. Fox (Ed.). *Models in Quantitative Criminology*. New York: Academic Press.

Harris, C. M. and Moitra, S. (1978). 'Improved statistical techniques for the measurement of recidivism'. *Journal of Research in Crime and Delinquency*, 15, 194–213.

Hindelang, M., Hirschi, T. and Weis, J. G. (1981). *Measuring Delinquency*. Beverly Hills: Sage Publications.

Hirschi, T. and Gottfredson, M. (1983). 'Age and the explanation of crime'. *American Journal of Sociology*, 89,552–84.

Hirschi, T. and Gottfredson, M. (1986). 'The distinction between crime and criminality'. In: T. Hartnagel and R. Silverman (Eds.). *Critique and Explanation*. New Brunswick, N.J.: Transaction Books.

Home Office (annually). *Criminal Statistics England and Wales*. London: HMSO.

Home Office (annually). *Prison Statistics, England and Wales*. London: HMSO.

Home Office Statistical Department (1985). *Criminal Careers of those born in 1953, 1958, 1963*. Statistical Bulletin 7/85. London: Home Office Statistical Department.

Home Office Statistical Department (1989a). *Crime Statistics for the Metropolitan Police District by Ethnic Group, 1987: Victims, Suspects and those Arrested*. Statistical Bulletin 5/89. London: Home Office Statistical Department.

Home Office Statistical Department (1989b). Criminal and Custodial Careers of those born in 1953, 1958 and 1963. Statistical Bulletin 32/89. London: Home Office Statistical Department.

Home Office. (1990). *Crime, Justice and Protecting the Public: The Government's Proposals for Legislation*. London: HMSO.

Hope, T. (1985). *Implementing Crime Prevention Measures*. Home Office Research Study No. 86. London: HMSO.

Hope, T. and Shaw, M. (1988). *Communities and Crime Reduction*. London: HMSO.

Jagger, C. and Clayton, D. G. (1981). 'Fitting Cox's regression model to censored survival data'. *GLIM Newsletter* No. 5, 38–44.

Jamison, R. N. (1977). *Personality, Anti-social Behaviour and Risk Perception in Adolescents*. Paper delivered to the British Psychological Society, London.

Jarvis, G. and Parker, H. (1989). 'Young heroin users and crime'. *British Journal of Criminology*, 29, 175–85.

Karger, T and Sutterer, P. (1988). 'On longitudinal research in criminology and the first results from the Freiburg Cohort Study'. In: G. Kaiser and I. Geissler (Eds.). *Crime and Criminal Justice*. Criminological Research Report No. 36. Freiburg: Max Planck Institute.

Kempf, K. L. (1987). 'Specialization and the criminal career'. *Criminology*, 25, 399–420.

Kitsuse, J. and Cicourel, A. (1963). 'A note on the use of official statistics'. *Social Problems*, 11, 131–9.

Klein, M. W. (1984). 'Offence specialisation and versitility among juveniles'. *British Journal of Criminology*, 24,185–194.

Klein, M. W. (1989). *Cross-National Research in Self-Reported Crime and Delinquency*. Dordrecht, The Netherlands: Kluwer Academic Publishers.

Knight, B. J. and West, D. J. (1975). 'Temporary and continuing delinquency'. *British Journal of Criminology*, 15, 43–50.

Lab, S. P. (1984). 'Patterns in juvenile misbehavior'. *Crime and Delinquency*, 30, 293–308.

Lambert, J. (1970). *Crime, Police and Race Relations*. London: Oxford University Press.

Laycock, G. and Tarling, R. (1985). 'Police force cautioning: policy and practice'. *The Howard Journal of Criminal Justice*, 24, 81–92.

Lewis, C., Newson, E. and Newson, J. (1982). 'Father participation through childhood and its relationship with career aspirations and delinquency'. In: Beail, N. and McGuire, J. (Eds.). *Fathers, Psychological Perspectives*. London: Junction Books.

Linster, R. L. and Patterson, E. B. (1987). *Probability Models of Recidivism: An exploration*. Discussion Paper 3–87. Washington D.C.: National Institute of Justice.

Little, A. (1965). 'The "Prevalance" of recorded delinquency and recidivism in England and Wales'. *American Sociological Review*, 30,

260–3.

Loeber, R. and Dishion, T. (1983). 'Early predictiors of male delinquency: a review'. *Psychological Bulletin*, 94, 68–99.

McClintock, F. H. and Avison, N. H. (1968). *Crime in England and Wales*. London: Heinemann.

Maltz, M. D. (1984). *Recidivism*. Orlando, FL: Academic Press.

Maltz, M. D. and McCleary, R. (1977). 'The mathematics of behavioral change: Recidivism and construct validity'. *Evaluation Quarterly*, 1, 421–38.

Martin, S. E., Sechrest, L. B. and Redner, R. (1981). *New Directions in the Rehabilitation of Criminal Offenders*. Washington D.C.: National Academy of Sciences.

Martinson, R. (1974). 'What Works? – Questions and answers about prison reform'. Public Interest, 10, 22–54.

Mawby, R. (1980). 'Sex and crime: the results of a self-report study'. *British Journal of Sociology*, 31, 525–43.

Mawby, R., McCulloch, J. W. and Batta, I. D. (1979). 'Crime amongst Asian juveniles in Bradford'. *International Journal of the Sociology of Law*, 7, 297–306.

Maxim, P. S. (1986). 'Cohort size and juvenile delinquency in England and Wales'. *Journal of Criminal Justice*, 14, 491–499.

May, D. (1975). 'Truancy, school absenteeism and delinquency'. *Scottish Educational Studies*, 7, 97–107.

Mayhew, P. and Elliott, D. P. (1990). 'Self-reported offending, victimization and the British Crime Survey'. *Victims and Violence*, 5, 83–96.

Miller, F., Court, S., Knox, E., and Brandon, S. (1974). *The School Years in Newcastle-upon-Tyne*. London: Oxford University Press.

Mitchell, S. and Rosa, P. (1981). 'Boyhood behaviour problems as precursers of criminality: a fifteen year follow-up'. *Journal of Child Psychology and Psychiatry*, 22, 19–33.

Mott, J. (1973). 'London juvenile drug offenders'. *British Journal of Criminology*, 13, 209–17.

Mott, J. (1980). 'Opiate use and crime in the United Kingdom'. *Contemporary Drug Problems*, Winter, 437–51.

Mott, J. (1985). 'Self-reported cannabis use in Great Britain in 1981'. *British Journal of Addiction*, 80, 37–43.

Mott, J. (1987). *Alcohol and Crime in the United Kingdom*. Paper presented at the British Criminology Conference.

Mott, J. (1990). 'Young people, alcohol and crime'. *Research Bulletin* No.

28, 24–28. London: Home Office Research and Planning Unit.

Mott, J. (1991). 'Crime, heroin and licit supply.' In: D. K. Whynes and P. T. Bean (Eds.). *Policing and Prescribing: The British system of drug control.* London: MacMillan Press.

Moxon, D. (1988). *Sentencing Practice in the Crown Court.* Home Office Research Study No. 103. London: HMSO

Nagin, D. S. and Smith D. A. (1990). 'Participation in and frequency of delinquent behaviour: a test for structural differences'. *Journal of Quantitative Criminology*, 6, 335–356.

Nuttall, C. P. (1977). *Parole in England and Wales.* Home Office Research Study No. 38. London: HMSO.

Osborn, S. G. (1980). 'Moving home, leaving London and delinquent trends'. *British Journal of Criminology*, 20, 54–61.

Osborn, S. G. and West, D. J. (1979). 'Conviction records of fathers and sons compared'. *British Journal of Criminology*, 19, 120–33.

Osborn, S. G. and West, D. J. (1979). 'Marriage and delinquency: a postscript'. *British Journal of Criminology*, 19, 254–6.

Ouston, J. (1984). 'Delinquency, family background, and educational attainment'. *British Journal of Criminology*, 24, 2–26.

Parker, H. and Newcombe, R. (1987). 'Heroin use and acquisitive crime in an English community'. *British Journal of Sociology*, XXXVIII, 331–50.

Pease, K. and Hukkila, K. (1990). *Criminal Justice Systems in Europe and North America.* Helsinki, Finland: Helsinki Institute for Crime Prevention and Control.

Petersillia, J. and Greenwood, P. W. (1978). 'Mandatory prison sentences: their projected effects on crime and prison populations'. *Journal of Criminal Law and Criminology*, 69, 604–15.

Peterson, M. A. and Braiker, H. B. (1980). *Doing Crime: A Survey of California Prison Inmates.* Santa Monica, Calif: Rand Corporation.

Peterson, M. A. et al. (1982). *Survey of Prison and Jail Inmates: Background and Method.* Santa Monica, Calif: Rand Corporation.

Phillpotts, G. J. O. and Lancucki, L. B. (1979). *Previous Convictions, Sentence and Reconviction.* Home Office Research Study No. 53. London: HMSO.

Ramsay, M. (1982). *City Centre Crime: A Situational Approach to Prevention.* Research and Planning Unit Paper No. 21. London: Home Office Research and Planning Unit.

Reiss, A. J. (1986). 'Co-offender influences on criminal careers'. In: A. Blumstein, J. Cohen, J. A. Roth and C.A. Visher (Eds.). *Criminal*

Careers and 'Career Criminals'. Vol. II. Washington D.C.: National Academy of Sciences.

Reiss, A. J. and Farrington D. P. (1991). 'Advancing knowledge about co-offending: results from a prospective longitudinal survey of London males'. *The Journal of Criminal Law and Criminology*. 82, 360–95.

Rhodes, W. (1989). 'The criminal career: estimates of the duration and frequency of crime commission'. *Journal of Quantitative Criminology*, 5, 3–32.

Riley, D. (1984). 'Drivers' beliefs about alcohol and the law'. *Research Bulletin* No. 17, 32–35. London: Home Office Research and Planning Unit.

Riley, D. (1985). 'Drinking drivers: the limits to deterrence'. *The Howard Journal of Criminal Justice*, 24, 241–56.

Riley, D. and Shaw, M. (1985). *Parental Supervision and Juvenile Delinquency*. Home Office Research Study No. 83. London: HMSO.

Rojek, D. G. and Erickson, M. L. (1982). 'Delinquent careers: a test of the career escalation model'. *Criminology*, 20, 5–28.

Rutherford, A. (1986). *Growing Out of Crime*. Harmondsworth, England: Penguin Books.

Rutter, M. and Giller, H. (1983). *Juvenile Delinquency: Trends and Perspectives*. London: Penguin.

Schmidt, P. and Witte, A. D. (1984). *An Economic Analysis of Crime and Justice: Theory, methods and their applications*. Orlando, Fl: Academic Press.

Schmidt, P. and Witte, A. D. (1988). *Predicting Recidivism Using Survival Models*. New York: Springer-Verlag.

Sechrest, L. B., White, S. O. and Brown, E. D. (1979). *The Rehabilitation of Criminal Offenders: Problems and Prospects*. Washington D.C.: National Academy of sciences.

Shannon, L. W. (1981). *Assessing the Relationship of Adult Criminal Careers to Juvenile Careers.* Final report to the National Institute of Juvenile Justice. Iowa Urban Community Research Center. University of Iowa.

Shapland, J. M. (1978). 'Self-reported delinquency in boys aged 11 to 14'. *British Journal of Criminology*, 18, 255–66.

Shinnar, S. and Shinnar, R. (1975). 'The effect of the criminal justice system on the control of crime: a quantitative approach'. *Law and Society Review*, 9, 581–612.

Shover, N. (1983). 'The later stages of ordinary property offender careers'. *Social Problems*, 31, 208–18.

Sjoberg, L. (1978). *Broth, brottslinger och effekter inom rattsvagendet en systemanoly tisk studie*. Stockholm: TOS.

Smith, D. R. and Smith, W. R. (1984). 'Patterns of delinquent careers: an assessment of three perspectives. *Social Science Research*, 13, 129–158.

Soothill, K. L., Jack, A. and Gibbens, T. C. N. (1976). 'Rape – a 22-year cohort study'. *Medicine, Science and the Law*, 16, 62–9.

Stander, J., Farrington, D. P., Hill, G. and Altham, P. M. E. (1989). 'Markov chain analysis and specialization in criminal careers'. *British Journal of Criminology*. 29, 317–335.

Stattin, H., Magnusson, D. and Reichel, H. (1989). 'Criminal activity at different ages: a study based on a Swedish longitudinal research population'. *British Journal of Criminology*, 29, 368–385.

Stollmack, S. and Harris, C. M. (1974). 'Failure rate analysis applied to recidivism data'. *Operations Research*, 23, 1192–1205.

Tarling, R. (1982). 'Unemployment and crime'. *Research Bulletin* No. 14, 28–33. London: Home Office Research and Planning Unit.

Tracy, P. E., Wolfgang, M. E. and Figlio, R. M. (1990). *Delinquency Careers in Two Birth Cohorts*. New York: Plenum Press.

Tuck, M. (1989). *Drinking and Disorder: A Study of Non-Metropolitan Violence*. Home Office Research Study No. 108. London: HMSO.

Van Dine, S., Dinitz, S. and Conrad, J. P. (1977). 'The incapacitation of the dangerous offender: a statistical experiment'. *Journal of Research in Crime and Delinquency*, 14, 22–34.

Van Dine, S., Dinitz, S. and Conrad, J. P. (1979). 'The incapacitation of the chronic thug'. *Journal of Criminal Law and Criminology*, 70, 125–35.

Visher, C. A. (1986). 'The Rand inmate survey: a reanalysis'. In: A. Blumstein, J. Cohen, J. A. Roth and C. A. Visher (Eds.). *Criminal Careers and "Career Criminals"*. Vol II. Washington, D.C.: National Academy of Sciences.

Visher, C. A. and Roth, J. A. (1986). 'Participation on criminal careers'. In: A. Blumstein, J. Cohen, J. A. Roth and C. A. Visher (Eds.). *Criminal Careers and "Career Criminals"*. Vol I. Washington, D.C.: National Academy of Sciences.

Wadsworth, M. E. J. (1979). *Roots of Delinquency*. London: Martin Robertson.

Wagstaff, A. and Maynard, A. (1988). *Economic Aspects of the Illicit Drug Market Enforcement Policies in the United Kingdom*. Home Office Research Study No. 95. London: HMSO.

Walker, M. A. (1987). 'Interpreting race and crime statistics'. *Journal of the Royal Statistical Society, Series A*, 150, 39–56.

Walker, N., Hammond, W. and Steer, D. (1967). 'Repeated violence'. *Criminal Law Review*, 465–72.

Ward, D. (1987). *The Validity of the Reconviction Prediction Score*. Home Office Research Study No. 94. London: HMSO.

West, D. J. (1982). *Delinquency: Its Roots, Careers and Prospects*. London: Heinemann.

West, D. J. and Farrington, D. P. (1973). *Who Becomes Delinquent*? London: Heinemann.

West, D. J. and Farrington, D. P. (1977). *The Delinquent Way of Life*. London: Heinemann.

Wikstrom, P. H. (1987). *Patterns of Crime in a Birth Cohort*. Project Metropolitan 24. Stockholm: Department of Sociology, University of Stockholm.

Wilson J. Q. (1975). *Thinking about Crime*. New York: Basic Books.

Wilson, J. Q. and Herrnstein, R. J. (1985). *Crime and Human Nature*. New York: Simon and Schuster.

Wolf, P. (1984). 'Delinquent boys and family relations'. In: P. Wolf (Ed.). *Sequential Research*. Copenhagen: Department of Sociology, University of Copenhagen.

Wolfgang, M. E., Figlio, R. M., and Sellin, T. (1972). *Delinquency in a Birth Cohort*. Chicago: University of Chicago Press.

Wolfgang, M. E., Thornberry, T. P. and Figlio, R. M. (1987). *From Boy to Man, from Delinquency to Crime*. Chicago: Chicago University Press.

Wolpin, K. I. (1978). 'An economic analysis of crime and punishment in England and Wales, 1894–1967'. *Journal of Political Economy*, 86, 815–40.

Appendix 1: Indictable and standard list offences

Generally, attempting, conspiring, inciting, aiding, abetting, causing or permitting a crime is classified under the heading of the crime itself, though in certain cases it is shown separately.

Indictable offences

Violence against the person

Murder
Attempted murder
Threat or consipracy to murder
Manslaughter
Infanticide
Child destruction
Causing death by reckless driving
Manslaughter due to diminished responsibility
Wounding or other act endangering life
Endangering railway passenger
Endangering life at sea
Other wounding, etc
Assault
Cruelty to or neglect of children
Abandoning child aged under two years
Child abduction
Procuring illegal abortion
Concealment of birth

Sexual offences

Buggery
Indecent assault on a male
Indecency between males
Rape

Indecent assault on a female
Unlawful sexual intercourse with girl under 13
Unlawful sexual intercourse with girl under 16
Incest
Procuration
Abduction
Bigamy
Soliciting by a man
Gross indecency with a child

Burglary

Burglary in a dwelling
Aggravated burglary in a dwelling
Burglary in a building other than a dwelling
Aggravated burglary in a building other than a dwelling
Going equipped for stealing, etc

Robbery

Robbery

Theft and handling stolen goods

Theft from the person of another
Theft in a dwelling other than from automatic machine or meter
Theft by an employee
Theft or unauthorised taking from mail
Abstracting electricity
Theft of pedal cycle
Theft from vehicle
Theft from shops
Theft from automatic machine or meter
Theft or unauthorised taking of motor vehicle
Other theft or unauthorised taking
Handling stolen goods

Fraud and forgery

Fraud by company director, etc
False accounting. (Theft Act 1968, s.17)
Other fraud
Bankruptcy offence
Forgery, or use, of false prescription (in respect of drugs listed in Schedule 2 of the Misues of Drugs Act 1971)
Other forgery, etc. (including coinage and hallmarking offences)

Criminal damage

Arson
Criminal damage endangering life (excluding arson)
Other offences of criminal damage
Threat or possession with intent to commit criminal damage

Drug offences

Drug offences

Other indictable offences

Blackmail
Kidnapping
Treason Acts 1351–1842
Treason felony
Riot
Unlawful assembly
Other offences against the State or public order
Perjury
Libel
Betting, gaming and lotteries
Aiding suicide
Assist entry of illegal immigrant
Perverting the course of justice
Absconding from lawful custody
Firearms offence
Revenue Law offence
Failing to surrender to bail
Trade Descriptions Act and similar offences

Health and Safety at Work etc. Act 1974
Possession of obscene material etc
Protection from Eviction Act 1977
Adulteration of food or drugs
Public health offences
Other notifiable offences

Standard list offences

Standard list offences include all indictable offences listed above plus the following summary offences.

Summary offences

Aggravated assault
Assault on a consable
Brothel keeping
Cruelty to a child etc
Interference with motor vehicle
Indecent exposure
Summary offences of criminal or malicious damage
Unlawful possession
Found in enclosed premises
Summary drug offences
Summary immigration offences
Impersonating a police officer (subclasses 91, 92 and 93)

In addition, those motoring offences which are triable either way are treated as Standard List offences when dealt with at the Crown Court on indictment.

Appendix 2: Disposals awarded to 5,000 juvenile offenders

The table below sets out the number of police cautions (caut) and convictions at court (pros) awarded to 5,000 juvenile offenders born in 1963 who came to the attention of the Greater Manchester Police.

Number of times dealt with by the police	*Percentage of offenders*	*Number and type of disposal*	*Number of offenders*
1	66.0	1 caut	2271)
		1 pros	1029)
2	16.5	2 caut	64)
		1 caut & 1 pros	558)
		2 pros	202)
3	6.8	2 caut & 1 pros	45)
		1 caut & 2 pros	209)
		3 pros	86)
4	3.6	2 caut & 2 pros	24)
		1 caut & 3 pros	115)
		4 pros	39)
5	2.5	2 caut & 3 pros	20)
		1 caut & 4 pros	74)
		5 pros	29)
6	1.6	2 caut & 4 pros	14)
		1 caut & 5 pros	50)
		6 pros	16)
7	1.0	2 caut & 5 pros	8)
		1 caut & 6 pros	30)
		7 pros	10)
8	0.6	2 caut & 6 pros	10)
		1 caut & 7 pros	12)
		8 pros	6)
9	0.6	2 caut & 7 pros	5)
		1 caut & 8 pros	24)
		9 pros	3)
10	0.4	2 caut & 8 pros	1)
		1 caut & 9 pros	16)
		10 pros	2)
10+	0.6	2 caut & 10+ pros	0)
		1 caut & 10+ pros	23)
		10 + pros	5)
Total			5,000

AUTHOR INDEX

Subject index

Printed in the United Kingdom for HMSO
Dd296706 7/93 C9 G3397 10170